MARLENE VAN DER WESTHUIZEN

PHOTOGRAPHY BY GERDA GENIS

Sumptuous

FOOD FROM THE HEART OF FRANCE TO THE CAPE

Contents

ROMAN GATES & ONION SOUP   9

French onion soup, Entrecôte Beaujolaise, Cherry clafoutis, Veal cutlets with salsa verde, Potato & paprika bake, Chestnut & mushroom soup, Pork belly with star anise, cider & honey, Roly-poly with apricot confit

OF MARKETS & MEN   29

Terrine de campagne, Carrots with roasted walnuts in orange juice, Pâté aux pommes des terre, Green beans with anchovies & almonds, Une poule dans son pot, Luxe apple pies in custard crust, Pissalàdière, Chicken livers with prosciutto & roasted baby potato salad, Classic quiche Lorraine

BAGATELLE   49

Chicken liver pâté with port jelly, Spicy shoulder of lamb with aubergine caviar, Aubergine caviar, Cassis sorbet with ripe cherries, Butternut & leek soup, Lapin with saucisson, sage & smashed potatoes, Soufflé Grand Marnier, Crêtes & roupettes, Butternut & chèvre tartlets with pine nuts, Pot au feu with roasted potatoes & rosemary

BOUDOIRS, PEARS & CHOCOLATE POTS   73

Goat's cheese tarts with hazelnuts, Chicken with white wine, black olives & flambéed baby onions, Chocolate pots, Ripe pears smothered in tarragon hollandaise, Pan-fried lamb cutlets with Gruyère, Autumn cake with berries, Cassoulet, English pot pies à la David, Beef fillet

SUNFLOWERS & STATUES   95

Sardines oven-roasted, Quail with prosciutto & sage, White peach & basil compote, Duck breasts with green olive tapenade, Champagne jelly with berries, Melanzane Parmigiana, Potato, bean & prosciutto salad, Tomato and lamb stew ancienne, Malva pudding

MIDSUMMER DREAM   115

Chilled tomato soup, Lamb ribs with puy lentils & prosciutto, Puy lentils with prosciutto, Couscous with fresh parsley, Pistachio cake with Noble Late Harvest wine , Poached salmon with soubise, Endive with fennel & thyme, Champagne sabayon, French lamb shanks with tomato & Gorgonzola cream, Blinis Aux Jardins des Thévenets

ANTIQUES ON SUNDAY   135

Buffalo mozzarella with tomato, Grape & fennel seed tart, Tomato, chickpea & lentil soup, Venison tagliatelle, Salmon & egg pots, Chicken with pancetta, preserved lemon & herbs, Tarte au citron

STUDIO IN GREEN POINT   151

Spinach & sorrel soup, Succulent duck with ginger, chillies & coconut milk, Orange pudding from Ouma Mollie, Muesli from the Food Studio, Fresh figs with prosciutto & Roquefort cream, White fish with black olives & saffron sauce, Tea cake with glazed fruits, Poulet à la Lyonnaise, Fig & nut cake with creamy coffee icing

MIDDENS & VINES   171

Mozzarella salad with anchovies & capers, Seared tuna with pistou, tomatoes & black olives, Toasted tomatoes with pesto & Gorgonzola, Raan, Ricotta dessert with cognac & citrus zest, Asparagus with white anchovies, Red roman on the embers, Strawberries with Hanepoot

GODDESSES & GHOSTS   189

La soupe des vendanges, Beef tongue with caper berries & black olives, Blueberry pie, Venison fillet pan-fried with ginger & sage, Sweet potatoes with ginger & chillies, Poppy seed & orange cake, Creamy chicken with rosemary, Fabulous coffee cake

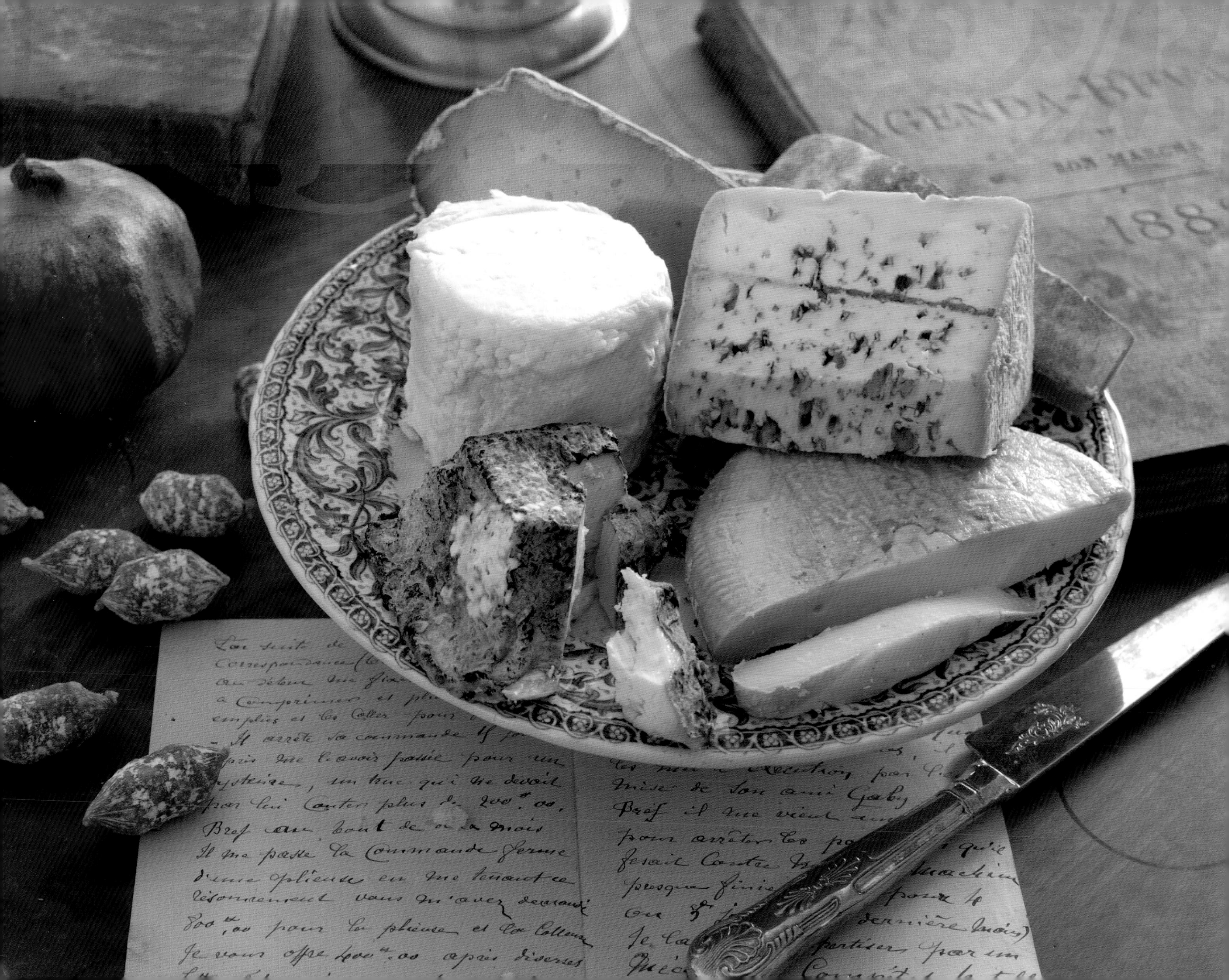

Preface

There was always going to be a second cookbook to trip down the little cobbled alley, past the apple orchard; perchance to explore what *Delectable* did not quite get round to. A book that was going to wrap up the story of a cottage in a tiny medieval village on top of a hill in the middle of France – a village where the rhythm of a day is measured by the peals from both the spire of the Church of Saint Sebastian and the bell above the 12th century Roman gate.

There needed to be a second book redolent of the fabulous food markets in the villages dotted around, and our contentment when filling our baskets with produce from the abundantly stacked stalls. This book needed to quietly pull together the dreamlike and sometimes discordant life I live between the kitchens of Bagatelle, Charroux, and the Food Studio in Green Point, Cape Town. And it needed to acknowledge the southern vineyards and the wild Indian Ocean that are so much part of our souls.

Hence, *Sumptuous*, where the journey continues with more of what I call 'brasserie luxe'. Simple, real food that requires very little guesswork. Platters piled high and served with generosity, and true pleasure, at tables laid amongst others, under a Bay tree in an old stone courtyard, or next to the crystal-clear fountain of a 17th century farmhouse, or on top of a 2 000-year-old midden overlooking a desolate beach near L'Agulhas at the southernmost tip of Africa. And to finish, a soupçon of excellent brandy ... distilled by a long line of goddesses and their ghosts.

I hope you will love the glimpse you'll get of the food and the places I adore. From old-fashioned tomato stew, malva pudding and quiche Lorraine to onion soup, pork belly, cassoulet, and even crêtes and roupettes! Boudoirs, ancient kitchens, rough luxe interiors, embroidered linens and old silver. The fabric of a life.

Marlene van der Westhuizen
Cape Town, 2009

CHAPTER 1

Roman gates & onion soup

The essence of the tiny hilltop village of Charroux is to be found not in the 12th century cobbled lanes, the hundreds of ancient wells, the ringing of the bells in the clocktowers, the wonderful little shops and tiny restaurants, or even in the generous portions of cassoulet that my elegant French neighbour tends to serve us; but rather in the month of September.

That is when, if you should cycle up the long, tree-lined drive towards the stone wall that marks the entrance to the village, the dry leaves gently lift around the wheels of your bicycle. And that is when, on your daily walk, you can fill your pockets with ripe chestnuts to be tossed into a warm pan later. In September you can easily crack the still-soft shells of the walnuts that you've gathered in one hand. They are completely sweet.

I adore breaking open a sun-warmed autumn fig, or smelling the pyramids of apples being wheelbarrowed to cosy kitchens to be dried or puréed to see us through the long winter. And all around the village, thin fingers of aromatic smoke from small leaf-burning fires leave a smoky haze in the sky. ♛

- French onion soup — 11
- Entrecôte Beaujolaise — 13
- Cherry clafoutis — 15
- Veal cutlets with salsa verde — 17
- Potato & paprika bake — 19
- Chestnut & mushroom soup — 21
- Pork belly with star anise, cider & honey — 23
- Roly-poly with apricot confit — 25

LEFT: *La Remise is the local deli in Charroux.*

BELOW: *The well in front of the museum.*
BOTTOM: *Charroux's mayor on his bicycle.*

ROMAN GATES & ONION SOUP

French
ONION SOUP

A typical French soup, without any extras … just as it should be.

Serves 8

- 6 large brown onions, peeled and thinly sliced
- 50 g butter
- 25 g flour
- 2 T fresh thyme leaves, stripped from their stems
- 2 cloves garlic, chopped
- 2 l good chicken stock
- salt to taste
- 3 T port

TO SERVE:
- 8 slices of white baguette
- 200 g Gruyère, grated

Fry the onions in the butter without allowing them to brown. When they are gloriously translucent with a subtle hint of caramel, sprinkle with the flour. Add the thyme. Continue cooking for a minute or two, stirring with a wooden spoon.

Add the garlic. Pour the stock gradually over the onions, stirring gently. Continue to cook for another 30 minutes over a gentle heat. Season, and flavour the delicious soup with the port.

In the meantime, switch on your oven's grill, cover the slices of baguette generously with the Gruyère, and toast until meltingly hot.

To serve, ladle the steaming soup into soup bowls and float a Gruyère toast on top. Utterly sumptuous!

TOP: *The Roman gate close to our cottage.*
ABOVE: *Fresh onions from the market.*

"A man seldom thinks of anything with more earnestness than he thinks of his dinner."
Samuel Johnson

ROMAN GATES & ONION SOUP

Entrecôte
BEAUJOLAISE

If you have ever wondered how classically trained chefs 'do' a steak … here you go!

Serves 2

- 2 T olive oil
- 2 sirloin steaks
- 2 T butter
- 2 shallots, peeled and chopped finely
- 125 ml dry white wine
- sea salt and freshly ground black pepper to taste
- flat-leaf parsley, chopped

Heat the oil in a frying pan. Sear the steaks quickly on both sides. Lower the heat and cook as required … preferably rare! Remove from the pan and keep warm.

Pour off the oil from the pan and toss in 1 T butter. When it's melted and 'hot', fry the shallots until golden. Pour in the wine and reduce by half.

Remove from the heat and incorporate the leftover butter in walnut-sized bits, stirring well after each knob has melted away.

Pour the sauce over the steaks, season, and garnish with parsley. Accompany with a fabulously creamy baked potato and a dollop of sour cream.

A glass of serious Cabernet Sauvignon will complement your meal well.

The cobbled street in front of our local mustard shop. This shop, which draws visitors from all over the world, has roupettes for sale.

ROMAN GATES & ONION SOUP

Cherry CLAFOUTIS

Clafoutis hails from the Limousin area of France and traditionally consists of black cherries arranged in a buttered dish, covered with a thickish batter and baked. We only wash and stalk the cherries and never remove the pips ... the kernels add their flavour to the batter during cooking. A wonderfully light cake that can happily be enjoyed with a glass of ice-cold rosé.

Serves 8

- 1 T butter for buttering the dish
- 250 g cake flour
- 125 ml castor sugar
- pinch of salt
- 4 eggs
- 1 t vanilla paste
- 500 ml boiled milk, cooled
- 2 T Stroh rum
- 750 g cherries*
- icing sugar

Butter a pie dish or any other pretty ovenproof container.

Mix together the flour, sugar and salt. Beat in the eggs, one at a time, and add the vanilla. Using a spatula, fold in the milk and rum.

Distribute the cherries evenly over the bottom of the dish. Pour the batter over the fruit and bake for about 35 minutes at 200 deg C/ Gas 6.

Dust with icing sugar before serving warm or cooled.

*Also lovely with peeled and sliced pears, peaches or with prunes.

Charroux boasts the prettiest streets and really old buildings. Some of these date from the 12th Century.

ROMAN GATES & ONION SOUP

15

ROMAN GATES & ONION SOUP

Veal cutlets
WITH SALSA VERDE

Veal cutlets are a little difficult to come by on sunny South African shores … but utterly delicious if you can convince your butcher to make a plan!

Serves 6

- 6 veal cutlets
- a handful of thyme leaves
- juice and rind of 1 lemon
- 125 ml dry white wine
- 300 ml extra virgin olive oil
- 1 bunch flat-leaf parsley, stems picked off
- 20 fresh basil leaves
- 20 small, crisp rocket leaves
- 1 clove garlic
- 6 anchovy fillets
- 1 T capers
- sea salt and freshly ground black pepper

Trim some of the fat from the cutlets … but leave a little; it really adds flavour. Place them in a large dish and sprinkle with the thyme, lemon juice and rind, wine and 100 ml of the olive oil. Season lightly. Cover and leave to marinate for at least an hour, though two hours is better.

To make the salsa verde, put the parsley, basil, rocket, garlic, anchovies and capers in a food processor and blend to a smooth paste. Add the remaining olive oil in a steady stream, continuing until emulsified.

Pat the meat dry and cook over a high heat in a very warm, oiled griddle pan. I love those little stripes … they make the dish look wildly professional!

Place one cutlet per person on a warmed plate, season, and spoon a dollop of fragrant salsa verde over the meat.

This dish needs a gentle Bordeaux.

ABOVE LEFT: *The Roman gate opposite the church.*
BELOW LEFT: *There are many ancient passages …*

TOP: *The secret entrance to the soap-maker's shop.*
BOTTOM: *Lovely soaps.*

ROMAN GATES & ONION SOUP

ROMAN GATES & ONION SOUP

18

Potato & paprika bake

This recipe is a family favourite that hails from my childhood days in Sasolburg. Maria Mayer is a Hungarian friend of my parents who used to cook this fabulous dish for us whenever we were invited for Sunday lunch on their farm. Very precious memories can be invoked with a yummy smell ... this is one of them.

Serves 6

- 2 T extra virgin olive oil
- 6 green peppers, pitted and sliced in rings
- 6 large onions, peeled and sliced in rings
- 5 cloves garlic, peeled and chopped
- 250 g bacon, cut into small strips
- 12 large waxy potatoes, cooked and peeled
- sea salt and freshly ground black pepper
- 12 eggs, hard-boiled, peeled and sliced
- 2 T paprika
- 375 ml fresh cream

Warm half the olive oil in a large pot. Combine the peppers, onions, garlic and bacon, and fry until the onions are translucent and the bacon just crisp. Oil an ovenproof dish with the rest of the olive oil. Slice the potatoes into thin rings and place a layer on the bottom of the dish. Dust with seasoning. Spoon a layer of the vegetable and bacon mixture on top of the potatoes. Add a layer of egg. Sprinkle liberally with paprika. Repeat until you have used all the ingredients, finishing with a layer of egg. Pour the cream over the dish and bake covered for 45 minutes at 180 deg C/Gas 4. This is excellent served with red meat.

ABOVE LEFT: *Pavanne, the Percheron, doing her bit for tourism.*
ABOVE RIGHT: *Cheeses for sale at La Remise, the local deli.*
FAR LEFT: *La Remise stocks a veritable feast!*

Chestnut
& MUSHROOM SOUP

To serve this soup you need a huge fire in the hearth, some good friends, a fresh, still-warm bread and, possibly, a wonderfully robust glass of Cabernet Sauvignon.

Serves 6

- 1 T olive oil
- 2 brown onions, peeled and chopped
- 2 medium potatoes, peeled and chopped
- 250 g chestnuts*
- 750 ml rich chicken stock**
- 2 T butter
- 250 g mushrooms of your choice, chopped
- salt and freshly ground black pepper
- 3 T crème fraîche

Heat the olive oil in a smallish pot, add the onion, and fry over medium heat until translucent. Add the potatoes, chestnuts and chicken stock, and cook until all ingredients are soft – about 20 minutes.

In the meantime, melt the butter in a small skillet, and allow it to brown to beurre noisette stage. Add the mushrooms to the skillet and fry at high heat until most of the juice has caramelised. Tip into the pot and stir well.

Purée in a food processor until completely smooth and wonderfully glossy. Season to taste and add more stock if it is a little too thick.

Return the soup to the pot and reheat to piping hot, then ladle it into soup bowls. Add a dollop of crème fraîche and garnish with a sliver or two of raw mushroom.

* The tinned chestnuts available at delis work well.
**Enrich stock by adding to one litre of chicken stock the following: 12 chicken wings, a peeled carrot or two, one celery stick, a clove or two of peeled garlic, a bouquet garni and about 500 ml water. Bring to the boil and cook until the meat comes off the bones. Pour through a sieve … and voila! – the most delicious, rich stock you can imagine. I love it!

FAR LEFT: *Corner in a busy kitchen.*
RIGHT TOP: *Chef enjoying a well-deserved cup of tea … should be wine!*
RIGHT BOTTOM: *Rose Thé is a favourite 'watering hole'.*

ROMAN GATES & ONION SOUP

ABOVE: *These tracks must lead somewhere.*

ROMAN GATES & ONION SOUP

Pork belly
WITH STAR ANISE, CIDER & HONEY

Fantastically satisfying to dig into. I love it!

Serves 6

- 2 T olive oil
- 4 spring onions, chopped
- 1 fat finger of ginger (or to taste), peeled and chopped
- 1 star anise
- 4 cloves
- 250 ml semi-sweet apple cider
- 125 ml honey
- 2 l chicken stock
- 2 fresh bay leaves
- 6 sage leaves, chopped
- 2 kg pork belly, bones removed, cut into bite-size pieces

Place the olive oil, spring onions, ginger, star anise, cloves, cider, honey and chicken stock into a large pot and bring to a simmering boil. Tip in the herbs and simmer for about 10 minutes. Add the pork, turn the heat down and cover. After about 30 minutes, remove the lid and cook, uncovered, over a really low heat, for another couple of hours, keeping an eye on it so it does not cook dry. Add some cider if needed. And have a glass or two yourself.

Once the meat is deliciously soft, spoon it onto a warm serving platter and keep warm.

Scoop most of the fat off the cooking liquid and discard. Reduce the rest of the liquid until it is thick and syrupy.

Spoon the sauce over the meat and serve accompanied by tiny boiled potatoes.

RIGHT TOP: *The gentle trees next to the graveyard.*
RIGHT BOTTOM: *Mme Sylviane Meunier in front of her pretty house next to the Church of Saint Sebastian.*

Roly-poly
WITH APRICOT CONFIT

This jammy, saucy pudding has been a family favourite for as long as I can remember. My brother, Gert Renier regularly used to put this together for 'something sweet' after a Sunday lunch.

Serves a family of 6 easily

- 125 g butter
- 500 g self-raising flour
- 5 ml vanilla paste
- 125 ml milk
- 250 g thick, glossy apricot jam, or to taste
- 500 ml cold water
- 250 ml castor sugar
- 125 g butter, cut into cubes

Preheat the oven to 180 deg C/Gas 4.

Rub the butter into the flour with your fingertips. Add the vanilla and milk, and fold together to form a soft dough. Roll out into a square on a floured board. The dough must be thinnish – about 2 to 3 mm. Spread liberally with the jam, then roll up like a Swiss roll and place in a buttered pie dish.

Pour the cold water into the dish. Sprinkle the sugar over the dough, then add the cubes of butter.

Bake for 90 minutes or until a glorious caramel colour. Cut in slices and serve with crème anglaise.

CRÈME ANGLAISE

- 500 ml milk
- 6 egg yolks
- 125 ml sugar
- vanilla paste

Bring the milk to the boil in a saucepan. Remove from the heat. Meanwhile, beat the egg yolks with the sugar until frothy. Slowly pour in the still warm milk … whisking furiously as you go.

Return the mixture to the saucepan and cook over a very low heat, stirring constantly, until it coats the back of a spoon.

Add the vanilla paste, set aside to cool, and serve with the pudding.

FAR LEFT: *There are almost 350 wells in Charroux.*
RIGHT: *A little lunch on the high street.*

*"The discovery of a new dish
does more for the happiness
of the human race than
the discovery of a new star."*
Anthelme Brillat – Savarin

The Belvedere, where you have the world at your feet.

LA FE
RESTA

CHAPTER 2

Of markets & men

Once a year, around the middle of July, there is a 'marche nocturne', or night market, in Charroux. Farmers come from all around to sell their produce from stalls rigged throughout the centre of the village and down the tiny streets; and a local folk-dancing troupe is responsible for some serious merriment.

Down the road from our cottage, Bagatelle, on the other side of the ancient stone well opposite the museum, you'll find La Halle. It was built around 1821 as a place where one could buy and sell wood. Young men looking for work would wait there for prospective employers to offer them a day job in the fields. Now, almost 200 years later, every Sunday morning during season, La Halle is transformed into a morning market selling delicious fruits and vegetables. You'll find artichokes, tomatoes, tiny sweet potatoes, haricots verts, crisp carrots and succulent fruits, as well as olives of every shape, colour and size. And what a delight to pick up some chèvre for a cheese platter …

- Terrine de campagne — 31
- Carrots with roasted walnuts in orange juice — 33
- Pâté aux pommes des terre — 35
- Green beans with anchovies & almonds — 37
- Une poule dans son pot — 39
- Luxe apple pies in custard crust — 41
- Pissaladière — 43
- Chicken livers with prosciutto & roasted baby potato salad — 45
- Classic quiche Lorraine — 47

Terrine

DE CAMPAGNE

Every girl should have a little terrine up her sleeve. This one is fairly simple and really good.

Serves 10 or so

- 20 g butter plus extra for greasing the terrine dish
- 125 g mushrooms, chopped
- 250 g bacon, cut in tiny slivers
- 2 onions, chopped
- pinch powdered cloves
- pinch grated nutmeg
- 2 t fresh thyme, chopped
- 2 t fresh sage, chopped
- 225 g pork loin, cut in tiny cubes
- 225 g veal, cut in cubes
- 225 g chicken or duck liver
- 3 cloves garlic, crushed
- 150 ml cognac or good-quality brandy
- 2 large eggs, whisked
- 125 ml cream
- sea salt and freshly ground black pepper
- bacon strips, enough to line a 2 litre terrine dish
- 225 g duck breast, fried in duck fat and sage, and cut in thin slices
- 225 g smoked ham or pancetta, cut in thin slices

Melt 10 g butter until it is golden and gives off a nutty smell (the beurre noisette stage). Fry the mushrooms until they are beautifully caramelised, and cooked fairly dry. Then scoop from the pan and set aside. Add the rest of the butter to the pan and melt. Fry the bacon slivers and onions until the onions are translucent and the bacon quite crispy. Add the cloves, nutmeg, thyme and sage. Spoon half of the mushrooms and half of the bacon-onion mix into a food processor; put the remaining halves of the mushrooms and bacon-onion mix into a mixing bowl.

Add the pork loin and veal to the mixing bowl with the mushrooms and bacon-onion mix.

Fry the liver with the garlic gently in the leftover pan juices until cooked but still pink on the inside. Add the cognac, bring to a fast boil and flambé. Spoon half of the liver and all the juices into the food processor to join the mushrooms and bacon-onion mix already in it. Process until smooth. Add the eggs and the cream, and process again. Season.

Cut the remaining liver into small cubes. Add to the rest of the ingredients in the mixing bowl, spoon the purée from the food processor into the bowl, and fold together to form a rough paste. Taste and season if needed.

Heat the oven to 180 deg C/Gas 4. Grease the terrine dish with butter, and line with the bacon strips, allowing them to fall over the sides of the dish.

(Turn page)

ABOVE: *Meat for sale!*
FAR LEFT TOP: *Olives at the Sunday morning market.*
FAR LEFT BOTTOM: *The Allier is famous for charcuterie.*

(Terrine de campagne continued)

Spoon half the mixture into the terrine dish and arrange the slices of duck and ham or pancetta on top. Add the rest of the purée and level perfectly. Fold the bacon over the filling to cover.

Cover the terrine dish with greased foil and put in a bain-marie in the oven for about 90 minutes. Remove from the oven and allow to cool. Remove the foil, put some waxed paper on top and weigh down – a couple of tins from the store cupboard works really well! Remove the weights after about 2 hours and place the terrine in the fridge for at least 2 days to allow the flavours to marry. To remove from the terrine dish, dip the whole dish in warm water for a second or two, gently pry the edges loose with a sharp knife, and tip onto a platter or cutting board.

Enjoy with a glass of Pinot Noir.

Carrots
WITH ROASTED WALNUTS IN ORANGE JUICE

This is possibly the most wonderful taste surprise I've ever had. Enjoy!

Serves 4

- 2 large, ripe oranges
- 300 g fresh baby carrots, peeled
- 100 g walnuts, chopped
- 50 g butter
- sea salt and freshly ground black pepper to taste

Thinly zest one of the oranges. Squeeze the juice from both. Place the carrots, nuts and zest in an ovenproof casserole and pour the juice over. Dot the carrots with the butter and season lightly. Cover and bake at 180 deg C/Gas 4 for 45 minutes, or until tender.

Serve with any white meat.

FAR LEFT: *Hunting for Sunday lunch.*

Pâté aux pommes
De Terre

A wonderfully satisfying dish from the Auvergne that goes down equally well in the Cape, especially during the wet winter months.

Serves 8

- butter for greasing the tart dish
- 2 rolls puff pastry, defrosted
- 1 egg, separated
- 50 g extra virgin olive oil
- 50 ml butter
- 8 leeks, sliced into pennies and washed
- 16 medium-sized potatoes, peeled and cooked
- 750 ml crème fraîche
- 175 g salad onions, chopped
- sea salt and freshly ground black pepper to taste

TOP RIGHT: *Cheese for lunch.*
BOTTOM RIGHT: *St Nectaire is an old favourite.*

Preheat the oven to 200 deg C/Gas 6.

Butter a tart dish and line it with a sheet of puff pastry. Prick the pastry with a fork, and then cover it with a thin film of egg white. This prevents the pastry from becoming soggy during baking.

Heat the olive oil and butter in a saucepan. Once the butter starts to foam, add the leeks and lightly fry them until tender. Keep aside. Slice the potatoes into thin, even rounds and tip into a large bowl. Season well. Add the leeks and half of the crème fraîche, and toss. Spoon into the pastry shell. Cover the mixture with the other sheet of pastry, and tuck it in neatly. Prick lightly with a sharp knife to allow the steam to escape. Bake for about 45 minutes or until the pastry has puffed out beautifully and is completely cooked.

In the meantime, gently stir the chopped salad onions into the remaining crème fraîche. Season.

Remove the pâté aux pommes des terre from the oven. Gently lift the top of the crust off the pie – and don't burn your fingers. You might need some help! Spoon the cold crème fraîche mixture onto the potatoes, return the top and serve immediately with a crisp green salad with heaps of avocado. This goes fantastically well with a glass of Sauvignon Blanc.

OF MARKETS & MEN

"The smell of good bread
baking, like the sound of
lightly flowing water,
is indescribable in its
evocation of innocence
and delight."
MFK Fisher

Green beans
WITH ANCHOVIES & ALMONDS

We all need to eat our greens. This is a good way to do just that!

Makes 6 small portions

- 300 g fine green beans, topped
- 50 ml olive oil
- 6 anchovies
- 3 cloves garlic, finely chopped
- 125 g almonds, slivered and roasted

Quickly boil the beans for about 4 minutes. Drain and keep warm. Heat the olive oil and anchovies in a small pan until the anchovies have melted away. Remove from the heat and add the garlic. Let it warm thoroughly.

Spoon this sauce over the beans, sprinkle with almonds and serve as a great side dish to any meat, brilliant with lamb!

FAR LEFT TOP: *The bakery in Charroux.*
FAR LEFT AND LEFT: *Breads galore!*

Une poule
DANS SON POT

In a text dating from 1664, the then Archbishop of Paris quotes a conversation between Henri IV of France and the Duke of Savoy in which the King uttered his famous words: "If God grants me a longer life, I will see to it that no peasant in my kingdom will lack the means to have a chicken in the pot every Sunday." Noble words indeed.

Serves 6

- 1 free range chicken
- 1 T olive oil
- 750 ml dry white wine
- 250 ml chicken stock
- 1 bouquet garni
- 2 whole carrots, peeled
- 4 whole courgettes
- 6 baby leeks, washed
- 4 cloves garlic, peeled
- 1 celery stick
- salt and freshly ground black pepper

Place the chicken in a large pot. Pour the olive oil over it … just for a bit of gloss! Add the wine and stock and bring to a gentle simmer. Add the bouquet garni, carrots, courgettes, leeks, garlic and celery.

Keep the pot simmering until the chicken meat is so soft that it is falling off the bones. Season generously.

Using a large ladle, gently lift the chicken out of the pot and arrange all the tender vegetables around it on a warm platter. This is comfort food at its best.

Eat immediately.

RIGHT: *Preparing dinner.*

OF MARKETS & MEN

Cooking is

"at once child's play

and adult joy"

Craig Claiborne.

Luxe apple pies IN CUSTARD CRUST

A glorious way to serve these little after-dinner snacks is to place a tot measure of Calvados in an elegant little glass on the plate next to the tiny puffs. I love the surprise factor!

Serves 6

- 1 roll puff pastry
- 1 T castor sugar
- 250 ml creamy mascarpone
- 1 t vanilla paste
- 2 eggs, whisked
- 6 tiny baby apples

Preheat the oven to 220 deg C/Gas 6.

With a cookie cutter, cut 6 small rounds of pastry and place them in a greased muffin pan. In a mixing bowl, fold the sugar into the mascarpone. Add the vanilla and eggs gently.

Spoon a dollop of this creamy mixture into the middle of each pastry round.

Place a tiny apple on top.

Bake immediately for about 25 minutes or until the pastry is a lovely caramel colour. Serve.

RIGHT: *Children at play during the marche nocturne.*
BELOW LEFT: *Justin Mesples.*
BELOW CENTRE: *Adeline Mosnier.*
BELOW RIGHT: *Antonin, twin brother of Justin.*

OF MARKETS & MEN

Pissaladière

The base is made with pastry dough and topped with shallots, garlic, courgettes, sliced tomatoes and oven-dried baby tomatoes. And of course finished off with anchovies. Fabulous!

Serves a fair number of guests … and some of the neighbours

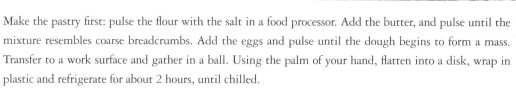

PASTRY

- 500 g plain flour
- ¼ t salt
- 125 g cold unsalted butter, cubed
- 2 eggs, beaten

TOPPING

- 6 shallots, peeled and chopped
- 4 cloves garlic, chopped
- 8 small courgettes, sliced in pennies
- 8 red tomatoes, sliced quite thickly
- 20 red or yellow baby tomatoes, halved and slightly oven-dried
- 10 tiny purple artichokes, cooked and halved*
- handful of fresh herbs such as basil, rosemary, thyme and sage, chopped
- salt and freshly ground black pepper to taste
- 20 anchovy fillets
- 250 g grated hard cheese (Cantal, Parmesan)
- extra virgin olive oil

Make the pastry first: pulse the flour with the salt in a food processor. Add the butter, and pulse until the mixture resembles coarse breadcrumbs. Add the eggs and pulse until the dough begins to form a mass. Transfer to a work surface and gather in a ball. Using the palm of your hand, flatten into a disk, wrap in plastic and refrigerate for about 2 hours, until chilled.

Roll out on a lightly floured surface to form a rectangle about 32 cm × 40 cm and about 5 mm thick. Transfer to a large baking sheet. Refrigerate again until the dough is firm … 10 minutes should be enough.

Now set the oven to 190 deg C/Gas 4. Scatter the shallots, garlic and courgettes over the pastry base. Arrange the sliced tomatoes in slightly overlapping rows inside the rim of the dough. Fill any gaps with the baby tomatoes and artichokes. Season with the herbs and salt and pepper. Decorate with the anchovies. Sprinkle with the cheese and olive oil.

Bake for 30 minutes in the top half of the oven. Then move the baking sheet down a notch and bake for another 25 minutes, or until the base is crispy. Let the pissaladière cool and cut into squares. Serve warm.

*These delightful little artichokes are available at the fresh produce markets around Charroux during April and May. They are virtually chokeless and just about bite size. If you can't lay your hands on any, use bottled artichokes. Quarter them into more manageable bits.

Chicken livers
WITH PROSCIUTTO & ROASTED BABY POTATO SALAD

This feeds my addiction to sage … again.

Serves 6

- small knob of butter
- 100 g prosciutto, sliced in ribbons
- 3 leeks, sliced in pennies and washed
- 500 g chicken livers, cleaned
- 25 ml brandy
- 50 ml olive oil
- 12 small potatoes, washed and boiled until just tender
- 20 sage leaves
- salt and freshly ground black pepper

Heat the butter in a small pan and quick-fry the prosciutto until crisp. Remove from the pan. Pat the leeks dry and fry till they are soft and lightly cooked. Remove from the pan and add the livers. Cook the livers lightly, taking care not to overcook – it's best if the livers are still slightly pink on the inside. Add the brandy to the pan, bring to a fast boil and toss a burning match in its direction. Don't panic if the entire pan catches fire … it's what you want!

Remove the pan from the heat (the flames will die away soon enough).

Spoon the livers into a dish and add the prosciutto and the leeks.

Add the olive oil to the pan juices. Re-heat. Slice the potatoes and add them to the pan. Cook until they are heated through. Add the sage leaves to the pan and warm. Toss the potatoes and sage into the dish with the livers, prosciutto and leeks, and serve!

LEFT: *All this and more to choose from.*

Classic quiche
LORRAINE

This is an original recipe that dates from the 1930s. And it is completely perfect.

Serves 6

- butter for greasing the pie dish
- 1 roll puff pastry, defrosted
- 25 g butter
- 350 g bacon, cut in tiny strips
- 4 eggs
- 350 ml fresh cream
- 6 T Gruyère, grated
- handful chives, chopped finely
- salt and freshly ground black pepper

Preheat the oven to 180 deg C/Gas 4. Line a buttered pie dish with the pastry. Prick the pastry lightly with a fork and keep cold.

Melt the butter in a pan and lightly fry the bacon strips until they are slightly browned. Beat together the eggs, cream, grated Gruyère and chives. Fold in the bacon, taste and then add a little salt if necessary. Grind some pepper into the mixture.

Pour into the waiting pie dish and bake for about 40 minutes. Serve with a small green salad and a glass of chilled Pinot Noir.

ABOVE: *Cheese and wine.*

CHAPTER 3

Bagatelle

To wake up behind the massive 15th century walls of Bagatelle, where the windows stay opened wide above the little cobbled street ... much to the consternation of the locals, who are perplexed by the typical Capetonian disregard for draughts! ... is one of my most profound pleasures. First there is the gentle calling of the church bells for early Mass; then, right on cue, you hear the light metallic clang of Mme Maenner's mustard shop's door being pushed open. Soon there is the much heavier sound of the massive wooden gates of the creperie, and the heady smell of fresh coffee.

Now you grapple for the loose change at your bedside, slip into something fairly respectable, clip your hair out of your face and trot off to the boulangerie, returning with a brown paper bag filled with warm croissants and a baguette for breakfast.

Around the hard pearwood table, born in the Knysna forests, many a wonderful meal has been shared. From breakfasts to main meals: tasty lamb, pâtés with port jelly, rabbits, soufflés, pork trotters and incredible local cheeses. Wine spills from vintages as far afield as the Dordogne and the Luberon have been laughed off over warm and wonderful nights of food and friendship.

And on a balmy evening you'll find us moving outside, to where a massive bay tree shields the courtyard ... 👑

- Chicken liver pâté with port jelly — 51
- Spicy shoulder of lamb with aubergine caviar — 53
- Aubergine caviar — 54
- Cassis sorbet with ripe cherries — 57
- Butternut & leek soup — 59
- Lapin with saucisson, sage & smashed potatoes — 61
- Soufflé Grand Marnier — 65
- Crêtes & roupettes — 67
- Butternut & chèvre tartlets with pine nuts — 69
- Pot au feu with roasted potatoes & rosemary — 71

Chicken liver pâté
WITH PORT JELLY

I love liver pâté but became really bored with the slightly sludgy look! Had to change it …
this is totally great!

Serves 12 as a snack

- 250 g salted butter
- 6 leeks, sliced in pennies and washed
- 500 g chicken livers
- handful of thyme
- 75 ml cognac*
- salt and freshly ground black pepper
- 1 large bunch of black grapes, halved and pitted

PORT JELLY

- 300 ml port
- 4 leaves of gelatine

Warm the port over a low heat. Soak the gelatine leaves in cold water for a couple of minutes and then add to the port. Stir until the gelatine has melted completely. Remove from the heat.

Melt half the butter in a pan and cook the leeks until soft. Add the livers, strip the thyme and add the leaves, and cook lightly (you want the livers to still be pink on the inside). Add the cognac. Remove from the heat. Add the rest of the butter to the mixture and, using a handheld liquidiser, process the mixture until completely smooth. Season.

Spoon into a greased earthenware bowl.

Arrange the grapes on top of the pâté. Spoon the cooled port jelly over the pâté and place in the fridge overnight.

You'll end up with an utterly glamorous pre-party snack!

Brandy will do nicely as well.

FAR LEFT: *Silver cutlery in a rural kitchen.*
RIGHT: *Under the bay tree in Bagatelle's courtyard.*

"I cook with wine ...
sometimes I even put it in food."
(Unknown)

Spicy shoulder of lamb
WITH AUBERGINE CAVIAR

This is a perfect main course: lamb with a creamy helping of aubergine caviar. Utterly sumptuous!

Serves 4

- 1 T sea salt
- 1 T coriander seeds
- 1 T fennel seeds
- 1 t freshly ground black pepper
- 125 ml extra virgin olive oil
- 1 shoulder of lamb
- 500 ml chicken or lamb stock
- 6 cloves garlic, peeled
- 500 ml fresh basil, chopped

Finely grind the salt, coriander seeds, fennel seeds and black pepper using a pestle and mortar. Blend the olive oil into the spicy mix and then rub it into the shoulder of lamb. And please use your fingers!

Bake the shoulder in a covered roasting dish at 180 deg C/Gas 4 for about 2 hours, or until succulently tender. Remove from the pan and keep warm.

Pour the stock into a medium-sized saucepan, add the pan juices and garlic cloves, and bring to a rapid boil. Reduce to a saucy quality. Add the chopped basil and serve immediately with aubergine caviar.*

This is wonderful with a Shiraz …

"Everything you can imagine is real." Pablo Picasso

* Turn page for this recipe.
FAR LEFT: *La Gatte wines from Bordeaux.*

BAGATELLE

Aubergine caviar

I spoon the caviar into lovely bowls and place them on the table between the guests. Everyone then serves themself. And almost all of them end up dipping their bread into it!

Serves about 10 people

- 2 medium aubergines, whole
- 2 T olive oil
- 3 cloves garlic, peeled and chopped
- 4 salad onions, finely chopped
- juice of 1 lemon
- 2 T flat-leaf parsley, chopped
- 250 ml crème fraîche
- sea salt and freshly ground black pepper to taste

Prick the aubergines all over with a fork and rub them with olive oil before roasting them at about 200 deg C/Gas 6 for 15-20 minutes, until completely tender. Remove from the oven, let them cool a bit ... for obvious reasons! ... then cut in half and scoop the flesh into a mixing bowl. Add the garlic, salad onions, lemon juice, parsley and crème fraîche and gently fold together. Season to taste and serve with the shoulder of lamb.

ABOVE: *Bagatelle's kitchen window at street level.*

RIGHT: *Sunset in the Allier.*

BAGATELLE

Cassis sorbet
WITH RIPE CHERRIES

Bribe the kids to remove the pips … then they're the ones who end up with the purple fingertips!

Serves 10 easily, with some to spare

- 1 kg fresh cherries, stoned
- zest of 1 lime
- 100 g castor sugar
- 1 t vanilla paste
- 50 ml cassis*

Place the stoned cherries in a bag in the freezer for at least 3 hours.

When they have frozen solid, tip them into a food processor together with the zest, castor sugar, vanilla and cassis, and liquidise until smooth. Scoop into a chilled serving dish and return to the freezer.

Remove the sorbet from the freezer a couple of minutes before serving. Wonderfully exciting with a glass of bubbly!

For a change, replace the cassis with grappa.

FAR LEFT: *At the market.*
ABOVE: *Furnishing an old house with brocante treasures is a complete pleasure.*

BAGATELLE

Butternut
& Leek Soup

I once, many years ago, invited the then French military attaché and his beautiful wife to our home for soup and sherry on a Sunday evening. My French was so bad that Mme completely misunderstood me, and they arrived elegantly dressed late afternoon on Saturday … just as I was drawing a bath for my own rather tacky person after spending an entire day replanting the courtyard garden! With ankles still caked in mud I laid a table in the kitchen and cooked this soup. It was delicious. The sherry helped …

Serves 6

- 50 g butter
- 6 leeks, sliced in pennies and washed thoroughly
- 1 kg sliced butternut
- 1 l chicken stock
- 2 cloves garlic, chopped
- 5 g nutmeg, grated
- sea salt and freshly ground black pepper
- crème fraîche
- sage, to garnish

Melt the butter in a large pot. Fry the leeks lightly until soft and translucent. Add the butternut to the pot and toss. Fry lightly.

Pour the chicken stock over the vegetables and bring to a gentle boil.

Turn down the heat and simmer until the butternut is completely cooked and tender. Add the garlic and nutmeg.

Remove the pot from the heat. Using a handheld liquidiser, whizz until it reaches a completely creamy consistency. Season to taste.

Serve in individual soup bowls, with a dollop of crème fraîche spooned onto each serving. Garnish each with a sage leaf.

BAGATELLE

Lapin

WITH SAUCISSON, SAGE & SMASHED POTATOES

If you're planning dinner and you're nervous about blackouts, this is the dish to choose – I've cooked this on top of the stove in my large Rosieres pot during just such circumstances. Thank goodness for a gas hob! I poured a bottle of dry white wine and 250 ml chicken stock over the rabbit and saucisson, and allowed the juices to gently reduce to a saucy consistency before serving with the potatoes. Wonderful!

Serves 6

- 1 rabbit, about 800 g
- salt and freshly ground black pepper
- 2 cloves garlic, chopped
- 2 T extra virgin olive oil
- 250 g saucisson, peeled and sliced thinly
- handful sage leaves
- 250 ml dry white wine
- 100 g cold butter, cut in small blocks
- 250 g chanterelle mushrooms
- 6 courgettes, julienned
- 2 medium, ripe tomatoes, peeled, pitted and diced

Pre-heat the oven to 180 deg C/Gas 4. Spread out the rabbit and rub with salt, pepper, a little of the garlic, and a little olive oil. Place the sliced saucisson in an ovenproof pan, dribble with the remaining olive oil, sprinkle over some of the sage leaves, and place the whole rabbit on top of it all. Cover and roast in the oven for about an hour, removing the cover halfway through, until the meat is succulently done.

Take out of the oven, cut the rabbit into serving portions, scoop onto a warm serving platter, and keep warm. Put the pan with the saucisson onto the heat, add a little of the wine, and quickly deglaze.

In the meantime, melt a teaspoon of the butter in a saucepan until it turns a light brown. Add the mushrooms and quickly fry until gloriously caramelised. Add the courgettes, the rest of the wine, the tomatoes, the rest of the sage, the rest of the garlic, and the pan juices and saucisson. Cook over a low heat for about 10 minutes, then whisk in the rest of the butter. Taste and season.

Spoon the thick sauce and all the bits and pieces over the meat and serve with a generous helping of smashed potatoes.

(Turn page for smashed potatoes.)

TOP RIGHT: *Chanterelle mushrooms have an excellent flavor.*

(Lapin with saucisson, sage & smashed potatoes continued)

SMASHED POTATOES

- 300 g young potatoes
- 3 T extra virgin olive oil
- sea salt and freshly ground black pepper
- handful flat-leaf parsley, destalked and finely chopped

Boil the potatoes in salted water until soft. Drain and return to the warm pot. Pour the olive oil over the potatoes and mash them … badly! … with a fork. Season, and stir the parsley into the potatoes, again using only the fork. A little dollop of butter is also quite perfect. Serve hot.

RIGHT: *Glasses drying on the ancient washstone in the kitchen.*

BAGATELLE

"One should either be a work of art
or wear a work of art."
Oscar Wilde

BAGATELLE

Soufflé GRAND MARNIER

My neighbour in Charroux, Marie-Chantel Bardet, serves this soufflé with great success to her guests ... and sometimes to us if we're lucky!

Serves 8

- butter for greasing ramekins
- 3 eggs, separated
- 70 g castor sugar
- 1 T Grand Marnier

Set the oven to 250 deg C/Gas 7 and allow enough time for the oven to heat properly. Butter 8 soufflé ramekins well.

Combine the egg yolks with the sugar and whip until light and creamy. Add the Grand Marnier and blend in thoroughly.

Whip the egg whites separately until they form a soft foam. Fold the foamy whites into the Grand Marnier mixture and gently divide among the ramekins.

Bake in the really hot oven for about 4 minutes, and serve immediately.

Crêtes
& ROUPETTES

In the tiny cobbled Rue de la Poullailerie, you'll find the mustard shop of Mme Simone Maenner on p.49. Among the more exclusive of the most exclusive delicacies for sale are the cockscombs and cock's oysters. Utterly delicious … and compulsory eating for all visitors to Bagatelle.

Serves … only the brave!

- 1 T olive oil
- 1 T chopped onion
- 125 ml Charroux mustard*
- 250 ml crème fraîche
- 1 clove garlic, chopped
- 300 g crêtes or cockscombs
- 300 g roupettes or cocks' oysters
- salt and freshly ground black pepper

In a small pan heat the olive oil and cook the onion until it is soft but not brown. Add the mustard and the crème fraîche. Heat this properly before adding the garlic and crêtes. Cook until the combs are completely soft. Remove from the heat and fold the oysters through the mixture. Season and spoon a tiny portion each into small bowls. You should be able to manage about 6 portions.

And I suggest that you serve this with something strong. A good cognac comes to mind …

* Or a mild creamy mustard of your choice.
RIGHT: *Just fabulous!*
FAR RIGHT: *Family at work … and play.*

BAGATELLE

Butternut & chèvre tartlets
WITH PINE NUTS

A match made in heaven. And do add the chilli.

Serves 6

- 1 roll puff pastry, defrosted
- 1 egg white
- 50 ml olive oil
- 6 leeks, sliced into pennies and rinsed
- 1 red chilli, chopped
- 6 × 5 mm-thick slices of butternut, oven-baked
- 6 slices chèvre
- 12 sage leaves
- salt and freshly ground black pepper
- crème fraîche
- pine nuts, lightly toasted

Heat oven to 220 deg C/Gas 6.

Line six oiled tart ramekins with pastry. Prick with a fork and brush with egg white.

Warm the olive oil in a pan, and fry the leeks and chilli until translucent but not browned.

Remove from the heat and allow to cool. Spoon into the tart bases, cover with a slice of butternut, follow with a slice of chèvre, and garnish with sage leaves. Season to taste and bake for about 15 minutes.

Serve with a small dollop of seasoned crème fraîche and a sprinkle of pine nuts.

These little tartlets are delightful with chilled Semillon.

RIGHT: *Using an old-fashioned rolling pin filled with ice water.*

...OT A...
Serves 8)

1 large ox tongue...
1 kg brisket, off the bone and...
2 pork trotters
750 ml dry white wine
5 leeks, sliced into pennies an...
1 head of garlic
bouquet garni
20 peppercorns
1 t dried fennel seeds
sea salt
juniper berries

Vegetables:
16 baby carrots, peeled
8 baby leeks, trimmed and w...
8 small courgettes, topped a...

To cook the the meat, place t...
bouquet garni, peppere... an...
wine and add cold... **Keep the** g...
the broth to boil. **Keep** the br...
liquid all the time. Once the bri...
the pot and keep warm. Allow t...
Skin the tongue and debone the t...
through.
In the meantime cook the vegetable...
in a saucepan with salted water whil...
Try to time the vegetables to be ready...

To serve... brisket, tongue and tro...
... er. Arrange the vegetables aound it. T...
with a bowl of aioli and some crusty bread!
Not to forget a glass or two of gutsy Shiraz.

BAGATELLE

Pot au feu
WITH ROASTED POTATOES & ROSEMARY

My dear friend, Marie Pierre Champagne, at whose lovely hilltop house in the Luberon I've spent many sun-warmed, lavender-scented days, cooked this for us one memorable holiday.

Serves 8

MEAT

- 1 ox tongue
- 1 kg brisket, off the bone and trimmed of fat
- 2 pork trotters, cleaned
- 5 leeks, sliced into pennies and washed
- 1 head garlic
- bouquet garni
- 20 peppercorns
- 1 t dried fennel seeds
- 750 ml dry white wine
- sea salt

VEGETABLES

- 16 baby carrots, peeled
- 8 baby leeks, trimmed and washed
- 8 small courgettes, topped and tailed

To cook the meat, place the tongue, brisket and trotters in a large pot with the leeks, garlic, bouquet garni, peppercorns and fennel seeds. Pour in the wine, and add cold water to cover, if necessary. Bring rapidly to the boil, then turn down to a slow simmer. Keep simmering for about 90 minutes, making sure it never boils, skimming off any scum that rises.

Once the brisket is soft enough to slice, remove it from the pot. Test with a sharp knife whether the meat is tender enough for your taste. Allow the tongue and trotters to continue cooking until really soft. Again you need to test for tenderness with a sharp knife.

When it's ready, remove the meat from the pot and skin the tongue. Return all the meats to the pot to warm through. Season to taste with sea salt.

In the meantime, cook the vegetables separately. The carrots and leeks can be cooked in a saucepan with salted water, while the courgettes are probably better off steamed. Try to time the vegetables to be ready roughly at the same time as the meat. You will need about 10 minutes ... and don't overcook the courgettes ... you want them slightly crunchy!

To serve, slice the brisket and tongue onto a large serving platter. Serve the trotters whole ... fabulous to barter for them! Arrange the vegetables around the meat. This truly authentic dish goes brilliantly with a bowl of aioli* and some baby potatoes.

And, of course, a glass or two/three of gutsy Shiraz.

Aioli is a wonderful, rich garlic mayonnaise.

ABOVE: *The sweetest baby potatoes in the world.*

CHAPTER 4

Boudoirs, pears & chocolate pots

Being caught in a sudden Auvergne downpour in the middle of one's daily constitutional is a fabulous excuse to flee to the cosy, foody kitchen of David and Colleen at La Grange du Belvedere. A gracious Bourbonnais farmhouse built on the outer fortifications of the original medieval City of Charroux, it is now a guesthouse filled with treasures gathered from unlikely places and brocantes.

As one races rather gracelessly through the 18th century gates and up the wet stone steps to the kitchen door, there is always a sense of expectation about 'what's cooking' on the massive stove in the corner ... and I'm yet to be disappointed. David's potted pies are a delight... but then so is everything else he has ever served us, like tiny quails' legs and salad.

To have a wonderful neighbour is one of life's true blessings. The sense of excitement, clouds of perfume and exquisite evening clothes worn by the groups of Bagatelle students, pay tribute to Mme Marie-Chantal Bardet's stylish generosity on the evening she hosts us in her lovely home, a short walk across the 12th century cobbles.

With a gentle, utterly sophisticated hand, Madame waves away any suggestion that anyone might be on a diet. Sinful portions of foie gras a la grandmere are dished up, accompanied by elegant glasses of Chateau Y'quem; then there are platters of cassoulet cooked with saussicon from Toulouse, beans from Albi, and confit de canard prepared over days by her childhood friend, Sylviane Meunier. And then, salad and bread, an Auvergne cheese platter and a to-die-for lemon soufflé.

As we stagger home, some of us barefoot by now, we know: life is good. ♛

- Goat's cheese tarts with hazelnuts — 75
- Chicken with white wine, black olives & flambéed baby onions — 77
- Chocolate pots — 79
- Ripe pears smothered in tarragon hollandaise — 81
- Pan-fried lamb cutlets with Gruyère — 83
- Autumn cake with berries — 85
- Cassoulet — 86
- English pot pies à la David — 89
- Beef fillet — 93

Goat's cheese tarts
WITH HAZELNUTS

A great starter to kick off with.

Serves 6

- 25 ml olive oil
- 5 young leeks, sliced into pennies and rinsed well
- 4 sprigs thyme, chopped
- 1 roll puff pastry
- 1 egg yolk, slightly beaten
- 6 slices of goat's cheese
- handful wild rocket
- 50 g hazelnuts, roasted and peeled
- 50 ml hazelnut oil

In the boudoir of Mme Marie-Chantal Bardet.

Preheat the oven to 220 deg C/Gas 6.

Heat the olive oil in a saucepan, add the leeks and thyme, and simmer gently, covered, for about 20 minutes, until the leeks are soft. Remove the lid, increase the heat, reduce the liquid, and cook until the leeks are slightly caramelised.

Using a cutter, punch 6 rounds out of the pastry and place them on a greased baking tray. Chill for about 10 minutes. Brush each round with a little egg yolk before spooning a dollop of leeks onto the middle of each round, leaving a border. Top with a slice of goat's cheese. Chill for 10 more minutes before baking for about 15 minutes in the hot oven.

Season lightly, and serve with rocket, a sprinkling of nuts and a dash of hazelnut oil.

ABOVE: *Enough spoons?*

Chicken
WITH WHITE WINE, BLACK OLIVES & FLAMBÉED BABY ONIONS

A dish I love to serve in winter … preferably in front of our fireplace!

Serves 8 generously

- 2 T extra virgin olive oil
- 1 T butter
- 8 organic chicken thighs
- 8 organic chicken legs
- 2 T plain flour
- 125 g black olives, stoned
- 2 cloves garlic, chopped
- 500 ml white wine
- 500 ml chicken stock
- 1 bay leaf
- 4 sprigs rosemary
- 6 sage leaves, chopped
- 500 ml water
- 1 t sea salt
- 24 baby onions, peeled*
- 1 T sugar
- 50 g butter
- 2 T good-quality cognac or brandy
- freshly ground black pepper

Bring the olive oil and butter to a fast sizzle in a large pot. Brown the chicken pieces, skin-side down, until lightly crisped. Sprinkle the flour over the chicken before turning the pieces over.

Toss the olives and garlic into the pot. Add the wine and chicken stock and bring to a gentle simmer before adding the bay leaf, rosemary and sage.

Cook the chicken until tender and succulent, about 1 hour, and then spoon the meat and olives into a large, warm serving platter.

While the chicken is cooking, bring 500 ml water to the boil in a smaller pot. Add the salt and pepper. Drop the onions into the water and boil until a sharp knife slips easily into the flesh, but they are still firm. Tip out to drain, return them to the empty pot, sprinkle with the sugar, and add the butter. Cook over a moderate heat until the sugar caramelises lightly and the onions are gloriously shiny. Have matches ready, pour the cognac over the onions and immediately light to flambée. Don't singe your eyebrows!

Pour the still-flaming onions over the chicken and serve with heaps of steaming basmati rice.

I love serving this with a masculine Bordeaux …

These are really easy to peel if you first pour some boiling water over them and allow them to cool a little before slipping off the skins.

ABOVE: *Flambéed …*

"*A woman has the age she deserves.*"

Coco Chanel

Chocolate pots

An old favourite looking all new in individual moulds. I always find comfort in remembered tastes …

Serves 6

BATTER

- 75 g butter
- 180 g castor sugar
- 2 eggs
- 2 T cocoa powder
- pinch salt
- 250 g self-raising flour
- 125 ml milk
- ½ t vanilla paste

SAUCE

- 325 ml boiling water
- 250 g brown sugar
- 2 T cocoa powder
- 1 t vanilla paste

Whip the butter and sugar together until pale and fluffy. Add the eggs one at a time, beating constantly. Sift the cocoa powder, salt and flour together and fold into the mixture. Mix well. Add the milk a little at a time, making sure to blend the mixture well. Add the vanilla.

Stir all the sauce ingredients together in a bowl. Keep stirring until the sugar dissolves.

Turn the oven on to 180 deg C/Gas 4.

Butter 6 ramekins and pour a little sauce into each. Follow with the batter: the ramekins should be about three-quarters full. Bake for about 30 minutes. The sauce will gradually bubble gently to the top of each pudding. Serve with a dollop of vanilla ice cream.

RIGHT: *Gentle rest is to be had here …*

Vignettes in Colleen's kitchen.

Ripe pears
SMOTHERED IN TARRAGON HOLLANDAISE

An extremely elegant starter to begin a dinner with.

Serves 4

- 1 egg
- 2 T tarragon vinegar
- 4 T castor sugar
- 140 ml thick cream
- 2 ripe pears, peeled and de-pipped
- butter lettuce to serve
- 5 ml paprika

Heat up a double boiler. Whip the egg, vinegar and sugar in the top half until the mixture is thick and foamy. Remove from the heat and fold in the cream.

For each serving, place half a pear on top of some butter lettuce, and spoon the sauce over it. Garnish with paprika and serve immediately.

Dreamy room full of secrets.

Pan-fried lamb cutlets
WITH GRUYÈRE

Every nervous newlywed girl needs to have one recipe she can trust for when her mother-in-law comes to dinner. My mom's was spaghetti bolognaise … this was mine!

Serves 4

- 50 g butter
- 8 lamb cutlets, trimmed
- 1 onion, chopped
- 1 T flour
- 200 ml dry white wine
- 2 t smooth mustard
- 100 ml lamb stock
- 125 g Gruyère, grated*
- 1 small gherkin, finely chopped
- sea salt and freshly ground black pepper

A moment of quiet in Marie-Chantal's peaceful garden.

Melt the butter and fry the cutlets in a warm pan on the stove until the fat is crispy. Do not overcook the meat. Medium-rare to medium is fine. Remove the meat from the pan and keep warm. Fry the onion in the pan juices until soft.

Mix the flour into some of the wine and add to the pan with the rest of the wine, mustard and the stock. Stir until the sauce has thickened. Allow to simmer a little before adding the grated cheese and gherkin. Stir until the cheese has melted. Taste and season. Spoon the sauce over the cutlets and serve.

You'll never want lamb cutlets cooked any other way!

A mature Cheddar is really good as well!

TOP: *My neighbour, Mme Marie-Chantal Bardet.*
ABOVE: *A moment caught …*

BOUDOIRS, PEARS & CHOCOLATE POTS

Autumn cake
WITH BERRIES

This is so good that all my friends have tasted it at least twice!

Serves 10, with possible seconds

- 180 g soft butter
- 500 g castor sugar
- 3 eggs
- 2 egg yolks
- 5 ml vanilla paste
- 350 g self-raising flour
- 1 small pinch salt
- 150 ml milk

SYRUP

- 100 g castor sugar
- 350 ml water
- 1 T honey
- 200 g assorted berries

Heat the oven to 180 deg C/Gas 4 and line a large bread tin with waxed paper. Grease well.

Beat the butter and sugar until creamy and pale. Add the eggs one at a time, and beat thoroughly before adding the yolks for extra richness. Add the vanilla. Mix the flour and salt, and stir in alternately with the milk until all is incorporated and the mixture is smooth.

Spoon into the bread tin and bake for about 90 minutes or until a skewer comes out clean. Allow the cake to stand for 15 minutes before tipping it out of the tin.

Meanwhile, prepare the syrup by placing the sugar, water and honey into a saucepan. Bring to the boil and reduce until it has reached a syrupy consistency. Add the berries briefly to the syrup before removing them with a slotted spoon and spooning them 'into' the cake. Reduce the syrup a little more before pouring it over the cake immediately. It's even better if you can manage this while the cake is still warm!

Serve with thick cream.

As an alternative, add 2 T finely grated lemon peel and the juice of 2 lemons to the cake mixture. Prepare the syrup with the same amount of sugar and water, but add 3 T lemon juice and roughly peeled citrus peels that have been caramelised.

BOUDOIRS, PEARS & CHOCOLATE POTS

Cassoulet

I leave you to read ... and cook ... this recipe in the words of my delightful neighbour, Marie-Chantal, who, with a lot of coaxing and various bottles of wine, had to worm the details from her friend, Sylviane. No small task to get to family recipes ... I understood everything perfectly and, I'm sure, so will you!

Serves 8

- 500 g tarbais beans (big white ones)
- 250 g salted pork belly
- 2 big onions, each studded with 4 cloves
- 1 bouquet garni
- 6 cloves garlic, peeled
- 1 carrot, peeled
- 1 saucisson à cuire (this type of sausage is boiled in a liquid; it is 100% pork)
- 2 T duck fat, plus extra for frying*
- 500 g pork shoulder, cut in medium-sized cubes
- ¾ litre chicken stock
- 40 g flour
- 4 ripe tomatoes, peeled and chopped really finely
- salt and freshly ground pepper
- 4 saucisses de Toulouse (pork also, just smaller and they need to be fried)
- 500 g confit de canard**
- breadcrumbs

The day before, put the beans in unsalted cold water.

The next day, boil the beans, pork belly, onion with cloves, bouquet garni, garlic cloves and carrot. Water must truly cover everything. Boil slowly for 1½ hours (taste the beans).

Twenty minutes before the beans are ready, add the saucisson to the boiling beans.

Melt 2 big tablespoons of duck fat and brown the cubes of pork shoulder until golden brown, then take them out of the casserole. In the casserole, prepare a 'roux brun'*** with the stock and the flour. Add the tomato pulp.

Add salt and pepper (not too much salt), put back the pork shoulder cubes and allow to simmer for 2 hours.

Brown the saucisses de Toulouse in a tiny bit of duck fat.

In the oven, heated to around 200 deg C/Gas 6, lay the pieces of confit on the 'grille' (my source could not find any other word to describe the oven shelf) until they lose their fat and become crispy (about 20 minutes).

Strain the beans and keep the 'jus de cuisson' (use as a stock).

Cut the saucisson in big slices. Set up a terracotta dish with the beans and all the meat on top, and cover with the 'roux brun' and a little of the saved stock. See if there is enough seasoning. Sprinkle the breadcrumbs on top and cook in the oven au gratin.****

Finish the cassoulet, lay on your bed and refuse to eat for two days!!!

It can be prepared one day before and cooked au gratin before serving.

*duck fat: used to preserve and cook food. Can be found at some of our delis, or make your own!
**confit de canard: duck cooked in its own fat and stored in a pot, covered in the same fat to preserve it.
***roux brun: a cooked mixture of equal amounts of flour and butter or pan juices, used to thicken sauce.
****au gratin: a dish coated with breadcrumbs or cheese to form a protective layer that prevents the dish from drying out.

TOP: *In the herb garden outside Ebreuil.*
ABOVE: *Saucisson at the market in Bellenaves.*

BOUDOIRS, PEARS & CHOCOLATE POTS

ABOVE: *My kingdom for a SMEG!*

RIGHT: *David's pies in their rustic kitchen*

BOUDOIRS, PEARS & CHOCOLATE POTS

ENGLISH

Pot pies

À LA DAVID

According to my English neighbour, David, it is vitally important to make the stock ahead of time, and the pastry last.

Serves 12

JELLIED STOCK

- 3 or 4 medium-sized pork trotters
- trimmings from the pork belly
- 1 onion, peeled and chopped
- 1 carrot, peeled and sliced
- 1 bay leaf
- a little parsley, roughly chopped
- salt and freshly ground pepper

Place all the ingredients in a pot, cover with water and simmer for about 2 hours. Sieve, season with salt and pepper, and reduce further until it forms a jelly when cold.

BASIC PORK PIE MIX

- 14 g butter
- 1 onion, finely chopped
- ½ t each of fresh sage, fresh thyme and ground mace
- ¼ t each of dry mustard and mixed spice
- 455 g pork belly, weighed without skin or bones
- coarsely ground salt and pepper

Put all ingredients through a coarse grinder.

PASTRY

- 170 g flour
- pinch salt
- 90 ml milk and 90 ml water
- 85 g lard

Sift the flour and salt into a bowl, and make a well in the centre. Place the milk and lard into a saucepan, melt the lard, and bring the mixture to the boil. Pour into the flour, working very quickly with a wooden spoon. Knead by hand to produce a smooth dough with a texture like putty.

Line twelve 7 cm × 5 cm deep moulds while the pastry is still warm.

To assemble

Preheat the oven to 200 deg C/Gas 6.

Fill the pastry moulds with pork pie mix to about 5 mm of the rim. Bake for about an hour or until the pastry is browned. Spoon the warm jellied stock over to cover. Top with any one of the following, and leave to cool: cranberry sauce, onion confit, mild blue cheese, or chutney.

(continued on p. 90)

English pot pies à la David continued...

Ring the changes

To make a **veal, liver and pork pie,** grind together 75 g each of veal escalope, calf or lamb's liver and pork belly, weighed without skin or bones. To this, add 2 rashers of streaky bacon, a clove of garlic, 1 medium leek, ½ onion, and a pinch each of ground cinnamon and nutmeg. Season with salt and pepper.

To make a **pork and leek pie,** grind together 75 g each of pork fillet and pork belly, weighed without skin and bones. Add a clove of garlic, 2 large leeks, an onion, ½ t each of fresh sage and thyme, and a pinch each of ground cinnamon and nutmeg. Season with salt and pepper.

For a **pork and apple pie,** you'll need the same meat base as above, into which you'll add 2 rashers of streaky bacon, 2 peeled and cored apples, 1 onion, ½ t each of fresh sage and thyme, a pinch each of ground cinnamon and nutmeg. Season with salt and pepper.

A **lamb pie** will need 455 g lamb cut from the fillet end of the leg. Add 1 onion, 2 T chopped parsley, 1 large leek, 1 T mushroom ketchup or mushroom paste, and salt and pepper.

RIGHT: *Stairway in a guesthouse filled with travel books.*

RIGHT: *A guesthouse filled with treasures and books.*

PARIS
MON AMOUR

LEE MILLER PORTRAITS

1914-1918
NOUS ÉTIONS DES HOMMES
JACQUES MOREAU

"I don't like food, I love it!
If I don't love it,
I don't swallow."
Anton Ego in Ratatouille

Beef fillet

A saucy fillet that is dreadfully easy to cook for a table of friends.

Serves 8

- 1 x 3 kg fillet of beef
- 75 g butter
- 15 ml sea salt
- freshly ground black pepper to taste
- 75 g celery, chopped
- 75 g carrot, peeled and chopped
- 2 T flat-leaf parsley, chopped
- 1 small onion, peeled and chopped
- 2 small leeks, sliced in pennies and washed
- 1 T lemon zest
- 2 cloves garlic, peeled and crushed
- 350 ml fresh cream
- 350 ml sour cream

Rub the meat with some of the butter and season. Heat the leftover butter in a large cooking pan. Add the celery, carrot, parsley, onion, leeks, lemon zest and garlic to the pan. Place the beef on top of the other ingredients in the pan and roast in a moderate oven, 180 deg C/Gas 4, for about 25 minutes until it is cooked but still rare. Baste the meat with the vegetable mixture before putting it on a warm platter. Keep warm. Strain the vegetables from the juices and remove most of the fat.

Pour the pan juices into a small cooking pot, add the fresh cream and reduce until really thick. Add the sour cream and warm thoroughly without bringing to a boil. Slice the meat into thick slices, and spoon the sauce over the meat.

I really enjoy the combination of small jacket potatoes and ripe avocado with the fillet.

Utterly delicious with a glass of Shiraz.

CHAPTER 5

Sunflowers & statues

En route to Vichy, we pass through Chantelle to pick up some marrow bones, a lovely terrine de campagne, and some general groceries from the epicerie opposite the Mairie in the main street; to eventually stop at the Wednesday market in the tiny village of Bellenaves. Once you've parked in the shade of the massive stone walls that circle the gardens of the chateau opposite the church, it is a gentle stroll down to the square where some delicious gathering ... and a little hunting ... takes place. We shop for deep red tomatoes, sweet-scented melons from Cavaillon, and tiny crisp radishes that we'll later crunch, rolled in the rich Sel de Guérande from Normandy.

Afterwards, we take the slow route through the bright yellow fields of sunflowers to Vichy, where – after a long lunch at the Michelin-starred Maison Decoret – it is advisable to take a stroll around the Parc des Sources. The still very fashionable spa town of Vichy, with its belle epoque structures and art nouveau-style opera, straddles the wide Allier River, also known as a European Wild River ... full of salmon!

During our gentle meander home, we pass the sentinel-like statue of Notre Dame de Retour, erected after all the World War II prisoners of war from Ussel, Senat and Taxat came home safely. ♛

- Sardines oven-roasted — 97
- Quail with prosciutto & sage — 99
- White peach & basil compote — 101
- Duck breasts with green olive tapenade — 103
- Champagne jelly with berries — 105
- Melanzane Parmigiana — 107
- Potato, bean & prosciutto salad — 109
- Tomato and lamb stew ancienne — 111
- Malva pudding — 113

TOP: *Friendly faces everywhere.*
ABOVE: *At the marketplace in Bellenaves.*

*S*ardines
OVEN-ROASTED

A delectable way to start an al fresco lunch or dinner.

Serves 8

- 10 ml olive oil
- 16 fresh sardines, gutted and rinsed
- 8 cloves garlic
- 5 ml Maldon sea salt
- 5 ml freshly ground black pepper

Heat the oven to 180 deg C/Gas 4. Oil a baking tray with the olive oil, pat the sardines dry, and place them in two rows on the tray. Sprinkle the whole garlic cloves around the little fish. Gently roast the fish and garlic for about 15 minutes. It is not necessary to turn them over.

Remove the tray from the oven, season the beauties with salt and freshly ground black pepper, and serve them immediately with a crisp green salad and a glass of Sauvignon Blanc.

TOP LEFT: *Behind the church.*
TOP MIDDLE: *Fresh sardines.*
BOTTOM LEFT: *Watermelon.*
BOTTOM MIDDLE: *The seller of escargots at the Wednesday market.*
FAR RIGHT: *I often serve these little oven-roasted tomatoes with a small salad.*

Quail
WITH PROSCIUTTO & SAGE

Quails are utterly delicious and widely available in the Auvergne. I pick them up at my local supermarket in Gannat, where they lie alongside pheasant and guinea fowl.

Serves 6

- 6 quails, cleaned and wing tips removed
- 18 thin slices of prosciutto
- 12 sage leaves plus a sprig for garnish
- 50 ml extra virgin olive oil
- 2 red onions, peeled and roughly sliced
- 2 cloves garlic
- 2 small carrots, peeled
- bouquet garni
- 300 ml chicken stock
- 300 ml of a serious red wine

Remove the rather oily pope's nose from each quail … I normally just snip them off. Place a slice of prosciutto and a sage leaf into the cavity of each quail. Truss each quail with a piece of string.

Cover the bottom of a large heavy-based pot with olive oil and fry the onions until slightly caramelised. Add the birds and lightly brown on both sides. Add the garlic, carrots, bouquet garni – add the last 6 sage leaves to the latter – and remaining prosciutto, and fry together for about 5 minutes.

Pour the stock and wine into the pot and bring to a slow simmer. Gently cook over a relatively low heat until the meat is almost falling off the bones.

Remove the birds from the pot and keep warm. If necessary, reduce the sauce to thicken. Season and pour over the birds. Garnish with a sprig of sage and serve with some creamy polenta.

Quails for sale in Gannat on Saturday.

"A man taking basil
from a woman
will love her always."

– Sir Thomas More

ABOVE: *The honey-sweet flat peaches of the Auvergne.*

White peach

& Basil Compote

A delightful summer dessert.

- 125 g sugar
- 250 ml sweet white wine
- 1 t vanilla paste
- 1 T honey
- 4 cling peaches, peeled and sliced (not too thinly)
- handful fresh basil leaves, roughly chopped

Using a non-stick wok or rounded pan, dissolve the sugar in the wine, then add the vanilla paste. Allow the syrup to reduce to 'big bubble' stage before adding both the honey and the peach slices. Cook, stirring gently, for about 3 minutes. Remove from the heat, add the freshly chopped basil leaves and serve immediately with a dollop of vanilla ice cream.

RIGHT: *Crossing the Sioule river.*
TOP: *En route to Vichy one drives past the old church of Cognat high above you on a hill.*

Duck breasts
WITH GREEN OLIVE TAPENADE

This makes for a lovely, elegant dinner. Lots of candles and roses …

Serves 4

- 75 g duck fat
- 6 shallots, peeled and finely sliced
- 4 cloves garlic, peeled and finely chopped
- 30 large green olives, stoned
- leaves from 1 bunch parsley, some sprigs of thyme, and a handful sage and rosemary, chopped roughly
- 75 ml extra virgin olive oil
- 4 duck breasts, scored with a sharp knife
- 5 leeks, julienned and washed
- 250 ml duck stock or rich chicken stock*
- 200 g hazelnuts, toasted, peeled and chopped roughly
- handful fresh basil to garnish, optional
- sea salt and freshly ground black pepper

Heat the oven to 200 deg C/Gas 6.

Melt the duck fat in a frying pan and cook the shallots over a low heat with the garlic until soft but not browned. Set aside to cool.

Reserve 10 olives and purée the remainder with the cooked shallots and garlic, adding the parsley, thyme, sage, rosemary and olive oil.

Smear the herby olive tapenade over the lightly scored duck breasts, making sure to rub the mixture into the cuts you've made. Using the same pan, turn up the heat and place the breasts skin-side down to quick-fry them. The fat will start cooking immediately. Keep going until the skin is lovely and crisp. Turn and cook on the meaty side for no more than 4 minutes. You want the meat to still be succulently pink.

Remove from the pan and put aside to rest.

Deglaze the pan with a little water, blanch the leeks lightly in the pan juices, slice the remaining olives into the pan, and add the stock. Reduce until you have a rich, thick sauce. Add the hazelnuts.

To serve, thinly slice the warm duck breasts. Spoon the leek and nut mixture onto warmed serving plates, and top each with a pretty layer of sliced duck.

Garnish with freshly chopped basil if you want to.

Serve with a glass of Pinot Noir.

For a rich chicken stock, see p 21.

TOP: *Eiffel's aquaduct between Gannat and Charroux.*
ABOVE: *St Bonnet's herbs.*

"*A single glass of champagne imparts a feeling of exhilaration. The nerves are braced, the imagination is agreeably stirred ...*"
Winston Churchill

Having a glass of wine in Vichy. With Hediard in the background!

Champagne jelly
WITH BERRIES

A festive and wonderfully light alternative to a Christmas pudding … in Cape Town that is.

Serves 4

- 750 ml Champagne
- 5 gelatine leaves, soaked in a little water
- 400 g mixed berries

Heat the Champagne gently and add the gelatine leaves. Stir until they have melted completely. Remove from the heat. Arrange some of the berries in 4 jelly moulds and pour enough of the liquid over the berries to just cover them. Place in the refrigerator for as long as it takes for the jelly to set. Keep the rest of the liquid outside the fridge. Remove the moulds from the fridge and repeat the process until you have used all the berries and Champagne.

Leave the jellies in the fridge until you need them.

Dip the moulds in warm water for a moment before you tip them over on the serving plates. They will gradually ease their way down!

Great with, naturally, a glass of Champagne. And, if you wish, a little coulis of puréed fruit.

Quiet moments around the Parc des Sources in Vichy.

Marlene van der Westhuizen

From: Peter Borain [peterborain@
Sent: 18 September 2008 10:27
To: marlenevdw@mweb.co.za
Subject: Melanzini di Parmigiana

Hi Marlene, Its so interesting to write
I have never thought of how much of any
but you know more about that and I'm su
are nonsense or not.

SUNFLOWERS & STATUES

You
      medium onion brinjals diced. I often
   1 3-4 med/large brinjals diced.
      3-4 400 gm cans Tomatoes
   20X 400 gm cans Tomato Paste
      Small can grated or thin sliced Mozzarella
   200 gm grated or thin sliced Mozzarella
      1/2 Cup flat leaf Parsley [Italian] fine
   grated
      1 Tsp dried Oregano
      1 Large cloves Garlic crushed, More if you
      1 Cup Basil leaves , torn
                  ground Black Pepper
                  mm thick cover
                  the salt can
                  stirring
                  bottom pot until soft. Add
                               well so the
                               black pepper,and
                               ature so remove

Melanzane Parmigiana

Peter Borain, the father of an old friend, is the creator of possibly the best melanzane dish I have ever had the privilege to enjoy.
Peter was in America when I needed the recipe, and he actually had to write up the ingredients of a dish he claims he normally just throws together ... took him ages!

Serves 8

- 3 medium aubergines
- 125 ml olive oil plus extra for greasing dish and frying onion
- 1 onion, peeled and finely chopped
- 2 large cloves garlic, crushed
- 120 ml flat-leaf parsley, chopped finely
- 1 T dried oregano
- 6 really ripe tomatoes, peeled
- 25 ml tomato paste
- salt and freshly ground black pepper
- 250 g thinly sliced mozzarella*
- 250 ml basil leaves, chopped
- 100 g Parmesan, grated
- 400 ml cream

*Peter prefers to use buffalo mozzarella,
but if you can't find any, use what you have.

Heat the oven to 180 deg C/Gas 4.

Slice the aubergines lengthwise in thickish slices. If they are fresh, as they should be, you do not have to go through the whole 'salt-and-drain' process! Do not peel. Fry in the olive oil until fully cooked and soft, and put aside.

Fry the onion in a medium pot until soft and translucent. Add the garlic, parsley and oregano and fry over a low heat for no more than 2 minutes. Do not burn the garlic. Add the tomatoes, tomato paste, a little salt and black pepper, cover and cook gently for about 35 minutes. If you find that you have excess moisture, remove the lid and turn up the heat a little to allow the liquid to reduce.

Use a baking dish with sides at least 60 mm high. Oil the dish using a little olive oil to prevent sticking and cover the bottom with a layer of aubergine. Follow with a layer of mozzarella, then basil and finally a layer of tomato sauce. Repeat until you run out of either ingredients or dish! The final layer is a generous sprinkle of Parmesan.

Bake for about 40 minutes.

Now for the bit that makes this Peter's own!

He lets the dish cool, then refrigerates for a couple of hours to make cutting easier. Then he portions the melanzane, wraps each portion carefully in some plastic wrap, and freezes until needed.

When he wants to serve this, he thaws and places as many portions as he needs in individual dishes. He heats them in a moderate oven, about 180 deg C/Gas 4, for 20 minutes. About 3 minutes before removing them from the oven, he pours 50 ml of cream over each, taking care not to burn the cream.

Serve the moment they come from the oven. Fantastic with a green salad.

ABOVE: *The Mairie in Chantelle opposite the butchery and the friendly grocer.*

SUNFLOWERS & STATUES

"Vegetables are
interesting but lack
a sense of purpose
when unaccompanied
by a great
cut of meat."
Fran Lebowitz

Potato, bean
& Prosciutto Salad

This is a truly great salad to serve at an alfresco lunch. I pair it with some chilled Merlot. Always spectacular!

Serves 6

- 1 kg baby potatoes, scrubbed, boiled and kept warm
- 2 handfuls of baby green beans, lightly cooked but still crunchy
- 1 bunch of chives, chopped
- walnut oil to taste
- 6 slices prosciutto, cut into narrow strips and lightly grilled
- Salt and freshly ground black pepper to taste

Toss all the potatoes, beans, chives and prosciutto together. Drizzle with the walnut oil, season and serve immediately.

ABOVE: *The statue of Notre Dame de Retour.*
LEFT: *Fresh prosciutto at the market.*

SUNFLOWERS & STATUES

Blood-red orbs. Perfect for a stew.

Tomato and lamb stew
ANCIENNE

A little trip down nostalgia lane. We all used to love coming home on a cold wintry day to the smell of this stew. I deeply suspect that we still do …

Serves 8 comfortably

- 2 T extra virgin olive oil
- 25 g butter
- 2 kg stewing lamb, preferably including some ribs and flank
- 1 T flour
- 3 red onions, peeled and sliced roughly
- 1 litre chicken stock
- 8 small potatoes, peeled
- 8 ripe tomatoes, peeled and sliced
- 5 cloves garlic, chopped
- a pinch of dried chilli
- 2 t sugar
- sea salt and freshly ground black pepper to taste
- a handful young, fresh basil leaves, optional

Heat the olive oil in a large casserole dish. Melt the butter in the warm oil and brown the lamb. Dust with the flour. Add the chopped onions to the pot and fry with the meat for about 5 minutes, and then pour the stock into the casserole. Bring the meat to a slow simmer and allow to cook gently, uncovered, for an hour before adding the potatoes, tomatoes, garlic, chilli and sugar. Simmer for at least another hour over a low heat until the meat falls off the bones. If necessary, add a little more stock or water.

Taste, season and spoon into a serving dish.

Garnish with the basil and serve with a steaming dish of basmati rice.

This would be delicious with a bottle or two of Shiraz.

TOP: *The Chantelle butcher who keeps me in marrow bones.*
RIGHT: *Inside the butchery.*
FAR RIGHT: *French lamb chops. Exquisite!*

Wednesday shopping in Bellenaves.

Malva pudding

This is on special request for my friends from the breathtaking guesthouse, Clos du Lethe, in Uzès, close to Avignon … a classic dessert from South Africa.

Serves 8

SAUCE
- 250 ml thick cream
- 250 ml milk
- 5 ml vanilla paste
- 125 g butter
- 125 g castor sugar

½ too much

PUDDING
- 250 g castor sugar
- 50 g butter
- 1 egg
- 250 g self-raising flour
- pinch salt
- 250 ml milk
- 1 t wine vinegar
- 1 T smooth apricot jam

Heat the oven to 180 deg C/Gas 4, and grease an ovenproof pudding dish.

SAUCE
In a saucepan, combine the cream, milk, vanilla paste, butter and castor sugar, and heat while stirring gently. As soon as it starts to boil, remove from the heat.

PUDDING
In a blender, combine the sugar and butter. Add the egg and blend well. Combine the flour and salt, and add along with the milk. Stir the vinegar into the jam and add to the mixture. Blend thoroughly and spoon the dough into the pudding dish.

Bake for about 35 minutes or until a skewer comes out clean.

Reheat the sauce gently and immediately spoon it over the Malva pudding. Allow the sauce enough time to soak into the pudding before serving it with a scoop of vanilla ice cream.

Utterly delicious!

As sweet as honey …

CHAPTER 6

Midsummer dream

Arriving at the tranquil guest farm, Aux Jardins des Thévenets, after a couple of months in Cape Town is one of my more precious moments. One crunches up the gravel drive to where my wonderful, wise friend Lynn waits in front of their glorious old farmhouse, a tray of glasses on the linen-covered table next to her.

On a beautiful day we'll stay right there, venturing into the vast kitchen now and then to fetch another course of fabulous fare.

And in midsummer we will stretch out in the cool, rough-luxe lounge under the picture-covered walls, reading, snacking on tiny soufflés and having quiet conversations.

This, of course, only when she and her husband Olivier are not busy with what I fondly call their structural archaeology project. The truth about living in a 17th century home is that careful and truly tender restoration work is needed to find the layered complexity that is the charm of old buildings, and to expose it and allow the old walls to tell their story.

Late afternoon, driving home after a delicious meal and fabulously rich conversations around the long table, I know I'm back in the Allier. ♛

- Chilled tomato soup — 116
- Lamb ribs with puy lentils & prosciutto — 118
- Puy lentils with prosciutto — 119
- Couscous with fresh parsley — 121
- Pistachio cake with Noble Late Harvest wine — 123
- Poached salmon with soubise — 125
- Endive with fennel & thyme — 127
- Champagne sabayon — 129
- French lamb shanks with tomato & Gorgonzola cream — 131
- Blinis Aux Jardins des Thévenets — 133

ON THE LEFT: *Daybed in the garden.*
RIGHT: *Marble bust in the sitting room.*

Chilled tomato soup

This country-style soup combines all the typical summer flavours and ingredients that epitomise a gentle meal in the Charroux countryside.

Serves 6

- 800 g slightly overripe tomatoes, skinned and seeded
- ½ cucumber, peeled and sliced
- 2 leeks, sliced in pennies, well rinsed and chopped
- 2 cloves garlic, chopped
- 4 red peppers, roasted, peeled, de-seeded and chopped
- 150 ml plain yoghurt
- Sea salt and freshly ground black pepper to taste

Liquidise all the ingredients except the yoghurt. Fold the yoghurt into the soup and season to taste. Chill for at least an hour before you serve this summery soup with a small green salad and some warm, crusty bread. I love adding a dollop of tapenade as garnish.

ABOVE: *The gatehouse.*
ABOVE LEFT: *The fresh-water fountain next to the kitchen door.*

MIDSUMMER DREAM

Lamb ribs
WITH PUY LENTILS & PROSCIUTTO

Using the lentils from Puy in the Auvergne is what we always do in Charroux. You can often find them in the better local stores, but any other lentils will still be delicious.

Serves 6

- 1½ kg lamb ribs, cut in half and French-trimmed*
- 100 g butter
- 100 ml dry white wine
- a few sprigs of thyme
- 4 cloves garlic
- 1½ l veal stock
- 12 baby onions, peeled
- 6 young carrots, peeled
- sea salt and freshly ground black pepper

Trim away any excess fat from the meat.

Melt 60 g of the butter in a deep pan, and sear the ribs over a high heat; then add the wine, thyme and garlic. Bring to a gentle boil and simmer until the alcohol has evaporated. You will smell when it has all gone! Add the stock and bring back to a gentle simmer. Cover and allow to simmer for about 2 hours, checking regularly that the stew does not cook dry (if things start to look serious, top up with a little more stock or water).

Meanwhile, melt the rest of the butter, and braise the baby onions until tender and glossy.

Add the onions and carrots to the stew, and cook for another 15 minutes before removing the lamb and vegetables from the pan.

Spoon into a serving dish and keep warm.

Scoop most of the fat from the cooking liquid, and then bring it to a vigorous boil, reducing it to a sauce-like consistency. Season to taste with freshly ground black pepper and sea salt, then spoon it over the lamb ribs.

Serve with puy lentils and prosciutto. **

Ask your butcher to "French trim" the lamb ribs.

ABOVE: *Aux Jardins des Thévenets.*
FAR RIGHT: *Drinks in Lynn's garden.*
RIGHT: *Friends around the table.*

Puy Lentils with Prosciutto

Serves 6

- 6 thin slices prosciutto, cut into narrow strips
- 50 ml extra virgin olive oil
- 500 g puy lentils, cooked
- thyme for garnish

Fry the prosciutto in the olive oil, then fold into the cooked lentils. Season after tasting. Garnish with freshly cut sprigs of thyme.

*"Cooking done with care,
is an act of love."*
Craig Claiborne

*Herringbone-patterned brickwork between walnut beams
in the dining room.*

Couscous
WITH FRESH PARSLEY

Feeds a heap of people deliciously. And it's so easy. Just always remember to get your hands in there. Couscous needs air!

Easily serves 10

- 500 g couscous
- 5 ml sea salt
- 1 T olive oil
- handful flat-leaf parsley, chopped
- 2 T spring onions, chopped
- 3 T pine nuts, lightly pan-toasted

An easy, fairly foolproof and really therapeutic technique to guarantee a heap of lovely, light couscous is to pour the dry couscous into a glass bowl, season with the salt, and work the olive oil through with a fork. Try to get all the grains oiled.

In the meantime, boil a kettle of water. Pour enough over the couscous to just cover it. I always judge the level just by sight … about half a centimetre above the couscous level will do it! Immediately cover the bowl tightly with cling wrap or a plate, and let stand for 15 minutes.

Remove the cover and gently fork the steaming couscous onto a warm serving dish.

Now for the fun part! Remove your rings and wash your hands. The idea is to 'get air' into the grains. Lift handfuls of couscous as high as possible without making too much of a mess. Gently rub the grains together to break up any clumps. The grains will fall back into the serving dish – feather light.

Once you have worked through all the couscous, gently fold in the parsley, spring onions and pine nuts. And please use your fingers!

I enjoy serving couscous with any really saucy lamb dish.

LEFT: *Red chair in the foyer.*
RIGHT: *Windowsill with orchid.*

MIDSUMMER DREAM

121

MIDSUMMER DREAM

Pistachio cake

WITH NOBLE LATE HARVEST WINE

A lovely classic cake to have in your repertoire. I love baking these old favourites.

Serves 10

- 6 eggs
- 175 g castor sugar
- 1 T orange zest
- 125 ml Noble Late Harvest wine
- 100 ml olive oil
- a pinch salt
- 150 g self-raising flour
- 125 g unsalted pistachio nuts, chopped, plus extra for sprinkling
- icing sugar for dusting

Preheat the oven to 180 deg C/Gas 4 and line a medium cake tin with baking paper, greasing it well.*

Separate the eggs, and beat the yolks with the sugar until pale and fluffy. In a separate bowl, whisk the egg whites until stiff.

Fold the zest, wine, olive oil, salt, flour, nuts and egg whites into the yolk mixture.

Pour the mixture into the cake tin and bake for about 20 minutes. Reduce the heat to 100 deg C/Gas1 and bake for another 20 minutes. Remove from the oven and allow to cool before removing from the tin. The cake will deflate a little; like a soufflé. Lovely!

Dust with the icing sugar and sprinkle with some more pistachios. Serve with a glass of Ambeloui Cap Classique.

*I actually prefer baking this in a ring tin. It has such a festive air!

FAR LEFT TOP: *Pathway between the trees.*
FAR LEFT BOTTOM: *Fat cat Fluffy.*
RIGHT: *Á table …*

"I've learned that
making a 'living' is not the
same thing as making a 'life'."
Maya Angelou

Poached salmon
WITH SOUBISE

Soubise is the name given to dishes served with either a béchamel or velouté to which an onion purée has been added, or even served with just the unadulterated onion purée. I adore serving the velouté variation with fresh white fish, although this version, using a delicious portion of salmon, is a stunner.

Serves 6

- 2 large onions, peeled and thinly sliced
- 175 g butter
- sea salt and freshly ground black pepper
- 1 T extra virgin olive oil
- 1 leek, sliced into pennies and washed
- 1 fennel bulb, trimmed, sliced and washed
- 1 clove garlic
- a few sprigs thyme
- 2 bay leaves
- 2 fish heads
- 1 l water
- 125 ml white wine
- 2 T flour
- a pinch of saffron threads
- 125 ml full cream
- 6 portions of salmon, or firm-fleshed fish

To prepare the soubise, place the onions in a saucepan with plenty of salted water and bring to the boil. Drain and add 125 g of the butter, salt and pepper. Cover and cook over a gentle heat for about 20 minutes.

In the meantime, prepare the stock. Heat the olive oil in a heavy-based cooking pan and fry the leek, fennel and garlic until softened. Add the thyme, bay leaves, fish heads, water and wine, bring to a simmer and cook for 20 minutes.

Drain the stock through a fine sieve or cloth and pour into a jug.

In a deep cooking pot, melt the rest of the butter and make a roux by adding the flour. Stirring constantly over a medium heat, add three-quarters of the fish stock until you have a thick velouté.

Fold the soubise into the velouté, add the saffron and cream, and allow the sauce to cook gently for a minute or two. Taste and season.

To cook the fish, pour the rest of the stock into a large pan and bring to the boil. Turn down the heat slightly. Slide the fish portions into the simmering stock and poach for about 6 minutes, taking care not to overcook the fish.

Serve in large soup plates. Place a portion of fish in the middle of each plate and spoon the delicious sauce over it. Garnish with a sprig of thyme and serve with tiny new potatoes and a glass of rosé.

RIGHT TOP: *Zwelethu Mthethwa on a faraway wall in France Profond.*
RIGHT BOTTOM: *A massive fireplace in the dining room.*

Endive
WITH FENNEL & THYME

The first time I ever ate this combination of vegetables was a year ago in a tiny little restaurant called Alfred just off the Palais Royal in Paris. I adored it so much that it has become a staple! And I've been back to Alfred and his restaurant numerous times.

Serves 8

- 2 endives, quartered lengthwise
- 4 fennel bulbs, trimmed and sliced lengthwise in slices
- 50 ml olive oil
- 8 bay leaves, plus extra to garnish
- salt and freshly ground black pepper
- 8 sprigs of thyme

In two small pans, heat about 1 cm salted water. Place the endives into one and the fennel into the other, and bring to a fast boil. When the water has almost reduced completely, add the olive oil in equal measures to the pans, and braise the vegetables lightly. Add the bay leaves to the pan with the endives.

Place 8 plates in a row and lift the vegetables with tongs onto the plates, mixing them elegantly. Season lightly with salt and freshly ground black pepper.

Top the endive and fennel with a bay leaf, garnish with the thyme, and serve either as a delicious starter or an accompaniment to a main course.

Armoire filled with kitchenware.

Champagne sabayon

I normally spoon the sabayon over any fresh fruit or berries I can lay my hands on. My husband loves hearing the 'tack-tack' of the whisk and normally opens a bottle of Champagne on cue!

Serves 8

- 5 egg yolks
- 4 T castor sugar
- 1 t vanilla paste
- juice of 1 lemon
- 150 ml Champagne

Whisk the yolks, sugar, vanilla, lemon juice and Champagne in a bowl over a pan of boiling water. Take care not to let the base of the bowl touch the water. Once the mixture is thick and creamy, spoon it over berries of your choice.
Serve immediately.

RIGHT: *Rough luxe lounge, a cool haven during summer.*
FAR RIGHT: Louis Jansen van Vuuren *by Oliver Chaulieu.*

"In water one sees one's own face;
but in wine one beholds
the heart of another."

(Old French proverb)

French lamb shanks

WITH TOMATOES & GORGONZOLA CREAM

The French in the Auvergne use orange peel with their lamb dishes. What a refreshing, delightful taste!

Serves 6

- 6 lamb shanks
- 1 carrot, peeled and sliced into pennies
- 1 celery stick, chopped
- 1 whole garlic bulb, halved and dribbled with 2 T extra virgin olive oil
- bouquet garni
- 1 red onion, peeled and chopped
- 5 ripe tomatoes, peeled, de-seeded and chopped
- zest of 1 orange
- 500 ml dry white wine
- salt and freshly ground black pepper
- puff pastry, defrosted
- 1 t butter
- 1 pear, cubed
- 6 T Gorgonzola
- gremolata*

Heat the oven to 180 deg C/Gas 4. Arrange the shanks in a deep baking dish and add the carrot, celery, garlic, bouquet garni, onion, tomatoes and zest. Pour the wine over and season. Cover and bake for 3 hours, until the meat is as soft as marrow.

In the meantime, cut the pastry into 6 × 8 cm rounds and place on a greased baking tray. About 20 minutes before the shanks are due to come out, pop the pastry rounds into the oven as well and bake until puffed and golden brown.

Melt the butter in a small frying pan and toss the cubed pear until it is slightly caramelised but still crunchy.

Make a hollow in each round of pastry and place each in the centre of a plate. Spoon some cubed pear and a dollop of Gorgonzola into the hollow. Add a hot shank to each, and spoon some cooking juices over and around the shanks.

Sprinkle with gremolata, loosen the roasted garlic cloves from the bulb, and use to garnish. Serve with a fabulous Cabernet Savignon.

To make the gremolata, mix 3 T finely chopped parsley, 1 T finely chopped garlic, 1 T finely chopped lemon zest and 1 T finely chopped orange zest together. Set aside until needed.

ABOVE: *Clock in the swimming pool room ... to time lengths?*

Blinis
Aux Jardins des Thévenets

I have my friend Lynn to thank for this easy way to sort out that most versatile of starter and dessert basics, the blini.

Serves 6

- 125 ml plain yoghurt, natural or Bulgarian
- equal amount of self-raising flour: use the empty yoghurt cup to measure
- 1 egg
- 1 T oil

Mix all the ingredients together in a small bowl and set aside for 20 minutes. Heat a heavy-bottomed frying pan well, add just a drop of oil, and spoon tablespoons of batter into the pan. As soon as bubbles start appearing, flip over and do the other side. You'll probably find you can do five or six at a time in an average-sized pan; by the time you've spooned in the last one, the first one is ready to be flipped.

For starters, serve with anything savoury (a classic version is salmon, sour cream and a little chopped dill) or, for dessert, with cream or yoghurt and fresh berries.

RIGHT: *A plate by Hylton Nel.*

"A man who drinks only water
has a secret to hide from his fellow men."
Charles Baudelaire

MIDSUMMER DREAM

133

CHAPTER 7

Antiques on Sunday

A brocanteur is an antique dealer who deals in all kinds of fabulous wares on condition that they are different, interesting, truly valuable or pretty.

With this promise ringing in our ears, we venture forth just about every Sunday – as early as the previous evening allows ….

We hunt and scour the little markets in tiny villages. Sometimes we find heaps of beautiful embroidered napkins, tablecloths, dishcloths and sheets, white and cream and an earthy greyish-brown. We find ancient postcards, paintings, sculptures, books and frames. There are Gien and Limoges platters and plates, teacups and saucers, and Christofle silver by the handful once you get into the hang of knowing what to look for.

You bargain and play, have a glass of wine to slake your thirst, and shop some more! At lunch, in every village, there is a surge – 'A table!' – to enjoy a simple and delicious meal with a tiny glass or two of cold, crisp rosé.

The best part is unpacking all the treasures once we're back at Bagatelle. Gloating is allowed. ♛

FAR LEFT: *Locals and tourists mingle at the brocante.*

- Buffalo mozzarella with tomato   137
- Grape & fennel seed tart   139
- Tomato, chickpea & lentil soup   141
- Venison tagliatelle   143
- Salmon & egg pots   145
- Chicken with pancetta, preserved lemon & herbs   147
- Tarte au citron   149

Buffalo mozzarella
WITH TOMATO

One of my favourite salads ... one that with a little tweaking can always be different ... and the same!

Serves 6

- 1 T extra virgin olive oil
- 20 small rosa tomatoes, halved
- sea salt and freshly ground black pepper
- some sprigs of thyme
- 2 fresh buffalo mozzarella*
- 20 small basil leaves
- 1 T capers

Heat the oven to 180 deg C/Gas 4.

Coat an oven pan with olive oil, toss in the tomatoes, and roast for about 30 minutes. Season lightly and set aside.

Remove the thyme leaves from their stalks and toss in with the tomatoes.

Using your fingers, shred the buffalo mozzarella onto a serving platter and tuck in the basil leaves. Spoon the tomatoes and capers over the salad and enjoy with a glass of Sauvignon Blanc.

*Any other mozzarella might let you down a little ...

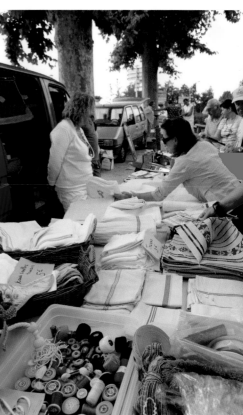

ABOVE: *Embroidery.*
RIGHT: *Dishcloths galore!*

Grape & fennel
SEED TART

I enjoy preparing this during harvest time ... for obvious reasons.

Serves 6

- 1 roll puff pastry, defrosted
- 1 egg white
- 2 whole eggs, whipped
- 125 ml crème fraîche
- 1 T castor sugar
- 1 t vanilla paste
- 400 g red grapes, stoned and halved
- 1 T fennel seeds
- thick cream to serve

RIGHT: *Old book and a handful of silver.*

Preheat the oven to 220 degrees C/Gas 6.

Line 6 greased, loose-bottomed (totally love this word ... and can't imagine why!) flan pans with the pastry, prick the dough with a fork, and brush lightly with a little egg white. This prevents the dough from becoming soggy.

Fold the eggs, crème fraîche, sugar and vanilla together.

Distribute the grape halves amongst the pastry bases and spoon the creamy mixture over the grapes. Sprinkle with the fennel seeds and slide into the oven for about 25 minutes or until the pastry is a lovely caramel colour.

Serve still piping hot with a dollop of thick cream.

Tomato,
CHICKPEA & LENTIL SOUP

What a delicious soup in which to drown your sorrows. My good friend, René, threw this together one cold, wet Saturday afternoon in Stellenbosch. We had it with a glass of their first-ever harvest ... Slee Eerste Oes Sauvignon Blanc. Splendid!

Serves 6

- 1 T olive oil
- 1 brown onion, peeled and chopped
- 250 g red beans, cooked
- 250 g lentils, cooked
- 250 g chickpeas, cooked
- 500 g tomatoes, peeled and chopped
- 1 carrot, peeled and sliced in pennies
- 2 cloves garlic, chopped
- 2 l chicken stock
- salt and freshly ground black pepper
- 2 T fresh parsley, chopped

Heat the olive oil in a large soup pot and lightly brown the onion before adding the beans, lentils and chickpeas. Give the vegetables a minute or two to braise gently in the olive oil before adding the tomatoes and carrot. Add the garlic and the stock and bring to a soft simmer. Boil the soup for about 10 minutes before removing it from the heat.

Pour half the soup into a food processor and pulse until it is completely smooth and creamy. Return to the pot and stir into the rest of the soup. Heat and season before serving with a generous helping of freshly chopped parsley.

Beautiful linen and other antiques.

Venison tagliatelle

This recipe is firmly aimed at the hunters among us. I always insist on stewing down all the carcass bones, salvaging as much of that succulent, tasty meat as possible. This is a fantastic way to use it.

Serves 6

- 8 whole tomatoes, peeled and puréed
- 1 T fresh oregano, chopped
- 1 T fresh basil, chopped
- 1 T fresh parsley, chopped
- 2 cloves garlic, chopped
- sea salt and freshly ground black pepper
- 500 g fresh tagliatelle
- 100 ml olive oil
- 500 g fynvleis or rillette*
- 250 ml crème fraîche
- 125 ml quince jelly

Stew the tomatoes in a large pot over a low heat for about 20 minutes, or until thickened. Stir in the herbs and garlic and simmer for another minute or two. Season to taste. Remove from the heat.

Cook the pasta in plenty of boiling, salted water until al dente. Drain and toss with a little of the olive oil.

Heat the rest of the oil over high heat in a large frying pan. Add the fynvleis, season to taste and fry until heated through – about 3 minutes. Reduce the heat and fold in the tomato sauce.

Serve the pasta in large bowls. Spoon the ragout on top of the pasta, finish off with a dollop of crème fraîche and serve the quince jelly on the side.

Tremendous food this!

*To make fynvleis or rillette, take all the bones that you can lay your hands on and place them in your biggest pot. I have an ancient 34 litre Rosieres, which is perfect. Add dry white wine to just about cover the bones, a handful of garlic cloves, a handful of rosemary, parsley and chives, and about 10 leeks. Also into the pot go some bay leaves, a couple of sprigs of thyme, 1 T dried coriander, 1 t juniper berries and about 500 ml olive oil. And to add interest, I throw in about 4 pork trotters.

Cover the pot and leave it in peace to simmer away for at least 4 hours, topping up with more dry white if needed. At the end of the cooking time, scoop the bones into a large dish (leave the juices simmering) and separate the meat. Do it by hand (gloves do come in handy). While you're doing this, the amazing stock is reducing to a wonderfully rich sauce.

Spoon the meat into plastic bags, each with a ladle or two of sauce which, when it cools, becomes a delicious jelly. Freeze what you don't use immediately. Fantastic for instant venison pie or, as here, ragout for pasta.

FAR RIGHT: *Small treasures are to be found.*
ABOVE: *Going patiently through stacks of porcelain.*

Salmon & egg pots

... for breakfast, naturally!

Serves 6

- a knob of butter
- 6 slices of smoked salmon
- 6 eggs
- 125 ml thick cream
- salt and freshly ground black pepper
- 30 ml chopped chives or salad onions

Preheat the oven to 180 deg C/Gas 4.

Butter 6 ramekins well, line them well with slivers of salmon and break an egg into each. Season the cream lightly with salt and pour it over the egg to almost cover. Sprinkle the top with the chives or salad onions, and place into a bain marie in the oven for about 8 minutes or until just set.

Remove from the oven and bain marie, give each a generous grind of pepper, and eat with warm toast.

"Wine is the most
civilized thing
in the world."
Ernest Hemingway

ANTIQUES ON SUNDAY

Chicken with pancetta,

PRESERVED LEMON & HERBS

What a gem of a chicken recipe! If you cannot find preserved lemon, just boil some fresh, sliced lemons until they are translucent. Almost as good as the real thing.

Serves 6.

- 125 ml extra virgin olive oil
- 1 T butter, plus 2 extra teaspoons
- 6 chicken drumsticks
- 6 chicken thighs
- 2 preserved lemons, sliced
- 500 ml white wine
- 250 ml chicken stock
- 250 ml each parsley, rosemary and sage, chopped
- 12 slices pancetta*
- freshly ground black pepper to taste
- crusty white bread to serve

Melt the olive oil and the tablespoon of butter together in a large pot. Brown the chicken pieces gently, and then add the lemon pieces. Pour the wine over, cover with the lid, and bring to the boil. After three minutes, add the stock and herbs. Bring back to a slow simmer.

Meanwhile, pan-fry the slices of pancetta in the remaining butter until crisp, then add to the simmering pot. Allow to gently cook for about 45 minutes, then season with freshly ground pepper. Serve when the chicken is succulently tender, and scoop up the tangy sauce with crusty white bread.

*Also truly magnificent with prosciutto instead.

Tarte au citron

Served warm and wobbly.

Serves 8

- 1 roll ready-made short pastry, defrosted
- 9 eggs
- 350 g castor sugar
- zest of 2 lemons
- juice of 5 lemons
- 250 ml thick cream
- 75 g icing sugar

Turn the oven to 180 deg C/Gas 3.

Grease a flan tin with a removable base, and fold the pastry into it. Gently use the knuckles of your fingers to ease the dough into the corners, allowing a small overhang (don't trim it off). Line with greaseproof paper and fill with baking beans (you could use dry lentils or rice). Bake for about 10 minutes, then remove from the oven and lift away the paper and 'filling'. Trim the dough and return to the oven for 10 more minutes, then take out and turn the oven down to about 120 deg C/Gas 1.

In the meantime, whisk the eggs with the sugar and zest until light and creamy. Stir in the lemon juice and then gently fold in the cream. Remove any froth before pouring into the hot pastry case. Bake for about 30 minutes or until the filling has set.

As you take the tart out of the oven, switch on the grill. Sieve the icing sugar over the tart and slide it briefly under the hot grill to caramelise.

Serve immediately.

CHAPTER 8

Studio in Green Point

Walking up the hill to the Food Studio in the early evening with my apron in one hand, key in the other, has become an integral part of my day. There is a sense of expectation, a tiny holding of breath every time I unlock the massive door and climb the steel staircase to the galley kitchen to prepare dinner. Once I've tied my apron tightly, and opened the kitchen doors on the balcony to let in the fresh breeze from the Atlantic, I pour myself a glass of wine and turn on the gas.

Green Point Village has a gentle rhythm that flows like the tides, in tune with the foghorn in the lighthouse which I can see from the Studio. We wait for the fishmonger to ring the doorbell twice a week … about two hours after the fruit seller has come by. Every second week, the dog-dip lady stops in front of the Studio – a wonderful sight with the Village dogs and owners patiently (mostly) waiting their turn.

Just down the road, on the corner, is the delightful Clyde Grocers where I can find almost anything. Pink and green marshmallow fish from an old-fashioned glass jar, shiny tomatoes and glossy magazines, and of course all the local gossip. Sometimes, a decadent slice of cheesecake from the adjacent Gran's Coffee Shoppe where one can sit at a tiny table on the pavement and watch the neighbourhood go by. 👑

- Spinach & sorrel soup 153
- Succulent duck with ginger, chillies & coconut milk 155
- Orange pudding from Ouma Mollie 157
- Muesli from the Food Studio 159
- Fresh figs with prosciutto & Roquefort cream 161
- White fish with black olives & saffron sauce 163
- Tea cake with glazed fruits 164
- Poulet à la Lyonnaise 167
- Fig & nut cake with creamy coffee icing 169

LEFT: *The table at the Food Studio.*

Spinach & sorrel soup

Undeniably one of the prettier soups I've seen. And healthier than most. In Charroux I pick the most flavourful sorrel when I go for my daily walk.

Serves 6 royally

- 75 ml olive oil
- 5 medium leeks, sliced into pennies and washed
- 2 cloves garlic, chopped
- 600 g baby spinach leaves, washed
- 300 g sorrel leaves, washed
- 1½ l chicken stock
- 150 ml crème fraîche
- 3 t horseradish cream
- salt and freshly ground black pepper to taste

Heat the olive oil in a large pot, add the leeks and cook until they are translucent and meltingly soft. Add the garlic, still-wet spinach and sorrel, and steam gently until the leaves have wilted. Add a little chicken stock – about 100 ml should be fine. Spoon everything into a food processor and whizz to a thinnish purée. Pour it back into the pot, add the rest of the stock, stir well and bring to a gentle simmer. Season.

In a little mixing bowl, fold the crème fraîche and the horseradish cream together.

Ladle the soup into individual soup bowls, garnish with a dollop of the creamy mixture and serve immediately.

ABOVE: *18 on Crox, a local B&B around the corner.*
ABOVE LEFT: *Artichokes ready for the pot.*

STUDIO IN GREEN POINT

"From wine,
what sudden
friendship springs!"
John Gay

Succulent duck
WITH GINGER, CHILLIES & COCONUT MILK

To die for. I once found a photograph of this dish with half of the recipe torn off. So I had to reinvent it … seems to work stupendously well though. Enjoy!

Serves 4

- 1 T duck fat
- 1 duck, cut into 8 portions*
- 4 shallots, peeled and chopped
- 4 cloves garlic, peeled and chopped
- 4 fresh red chillies, de-seeded and chopped
- 2 t fresh ginger
- 1 t turmeric
- 4 cardamom pods, husked and ground
- 1 stem fresh lemongrass, chopped
- 2 l coconut milk
- sea salt and freshly ground black pepper to taste
- basmati rice to serve

Melt the fat in a large pot, add the duck pieces, and fry over a medium heat until brown. Add the shallots, garlic, chillies, ginger, turmeric, cardamom and lemongrass. Stir-fry gently for about 2 minutes before adding the coconut milk. Bring to a gentle boil and simmer for at least 90 minutes, until the meat is deliciously tender, and the sauce wonderfully thick.

Taste and season.

Spoon the duck and sauce onto a warm serving platter and serve with basmati rice.

I enjoy a chilled Sauvignon Blanc from Bouchard Finlayson with this dish.

Wash the duck portions in cold water and rub each with white wine vinegar. Pour over boiling water and leave to stand for 5 minutes. The vinegar removes the slightly wild odour, and the boiling water melts some excess fat under the skin. Drain the meat in a colander and pat dry before you start to cook.

Orange pudding
FROM OUMA MOLLIE

Oranges are the main crop in the Gamtoos Valley in the Eastern Cape, where my grandmother was the Dutch Reformed dominee's wife. She called this her 'own concoction' and advised that, as this is a 'small pudding', it is better to either double or treble the ingredients for a big family. She signed the recipe 'Maria Murray van Rooyen'.

Serves 4

- 125 g castor sugar
- 100 g butter
- 50 ml sunflower oil
- pinch salt
- 1 egg
- 250 g self-raising flour, sifted
- 1 medium orange, peeled and pith removed

SYRUP
- 250 ml water
- 125 g castor sugar
- juice of 2 oranges
- 1 T orange zest
- 1 T good-quality brandy

Heat the oven to 180 deg C/Gas 4.

Blend the castor sugar and butter until creamy. Add the oil, salt and egg and mix well. Add the flour. Break the flesh of the orange into tiny pieces over the mixing bowl to catch all the juice, and fold into the dough. Spoon into a greased ovenproof baking dish. Bake for about 30 minutes or until a skewer comes out clean.

Meanwhile, make the syrup. Pour the water and sugar into a saucepan and bring to a slow boil, stirring until the sugar has melted. Add the orange juice and zest, and reduce for about 6 minutes or until syrupy. Add the brandy and pour the syrup over the lovely, crusty cake as it comes out of the oven. Serve with a crème anglaise or a scoop of vanilla ice cream.

"The cook was a good cook, as cooks go; and as cooks go she went."

Hector Hugh Munro

STUDIO IN GREEN POINT

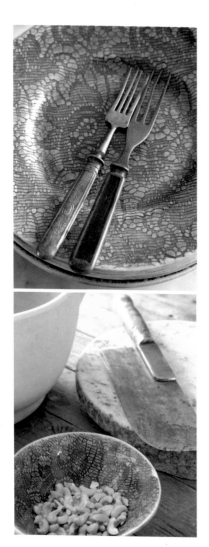

Muesli

FROM THE FOOD STUDIO

Our standard family breakfast. I sometimes mess around with the nuts, adding sunflower or pumpkin seeds, walnuts or even pine nuts. Just as you wish … it is always a fabulous way to start the day.

This quantity should last an average family about 2 weeks

- 750 g oats
- 750 g digestive bran
- 250 g desiccated coconut
- 100 g demerara sugar
- 250 g pistachio nuts, shelled
- 250 g almond flakes
- 500 g All-bran flakes
- 500 g Special K
- 500 g Hi-bulk bran
- 125 ml sunflower oil

Mix all the ingredients together in a large mixing bowl using a huge wooden spoon. Pour the mixture in four batches onto your oven pan, and bake at 180 deg C/Gas 4 for 15 minutes. Cool and store in dry, airtight containers. Enjoy with yoghurt or milk.

FAR LEFT: *Wonki Ware in the Food Studio.*
RIGHT: *Enjoying breakfast at Gran's Coffee Shoppe.*

Fresh figs
WITH PROSCIUTTO & ROQUEFORT CREAM

An utterly delicious starter.

Serves 4

- 125 ml chicken stock
- 125 ml cream
- 250 g Roquefort cheese, cut into blocks
- 4 slices prosciutto
- 4 ripe figs

Heat the oven to 180 deg C/Gas 4.

Bring the stock and the cream to a gentle rolling boil in a medium-sized pot. Once the liquid has reduced by at least half, add the cheese, stirring gently until it has melted and the sauce has the consistency of thick cream.

Meanwhile, roll a slice of prosciutto around each fig and place in an ovenproof dish. When the sauce is ready, spoon half of it over the figs, and keep the remainder warm. Bake the figs, uncovered, for 10 minutes. Remove from the oven, spoon onto serving plates and drizzle with the remaining sauce from the pot.

Serve with a glass of Chenin Blanc.

FAR LEFT: *David's Guesthouse, Green Point Village.*
RIGHT: *Catholic Church in the Village.*
FAR RIGHT: *Entrance to David's.*

STUDIO IN GREEN POINT

White fish

WITH BLACK OLIVES & SAFFRON SAUCE

I also enjoy preparing this with tuna, but any firm fish will do.

Serves 6

- sea salt and freshly ground black pepper
- 6 × 200 g fish fillets
- 2 shallots, peeled and quartered
- 1 clove garlic, peeled and halved
- 200 ml olive oil
- 2 pinches saffron
- 100 ml white wine
- 200 ml chicken stock
- 20 calamata olives, stoned
- 1 preserved lemon, thinly sliced
- a handful fresh flat-leaf parsley, chopped

Heat the oven to 180 deg C/Gas 4.

Season the fish fillets. Using an ovenproof pan, lightly fry the shallots and garlic in the olive oil over a medium heat. Add the fish and gently brown.

Soak the saffron in the wine for a few minutes before pouring both the wine and the stock into the pan. Add the olives and lemon slices. Bring to a low simmer, cover and transfer to the oven for 15 minutes.

Remove the pan from the oven, place the fish fillets on a warm plate, and quickly reduce the pan juices over a high flame until lovely and saucy. Spoon over the fish, garnish with parsley, and enjoy with a heap of tiny peeled and buttered young potatoes.

Conversations at the local

STUDIO IN GREEN POINT

Tea cake
WITH GLAZED FRUITS

A lighter and more colourful version of the English fruit cake we all eat around Christmas. I really like this one ...

Serves 12

- 100 g sultanas
- 75 ml sweet sherry
- 225 g peeled almonds, chopped roughly
- 225 g glacé orange and lemon peel, chopped
- 2 glacé dried green figs, chopped
- 10 glacé cherries, halved
- 200 g pine nuts, roasted
- 150 g dark chocolate, chopped
- 150 g castor sugar
- 125 g self-raising flour
- 1 t cinnamon powder
- 1 t allspice powder
- 3 cardamom pods, shelled and ground
- 50 g unsalted butter
- 3 eggs
- 3 T honey, melted
- heaps of different types of whole glacé fruit to decorate the cake

Preheat the oven to 180 deg C/Gas 4. Generously grease a medium cake tin – preferably a loose-bottomed one. Some baking paper lining might also help!

Soak the sultanas in the sherry overnight. Place the sultanas, any remaining sherry, almonds, orange and lemon peel, figs, cherries, pine nuts and chocolate in a large bowl. Add the sugar. Mix carefully. Sift the flour, cinnamon and allspice into a separate bowl. Add the cardamom. Tip these dry ingredients into the fruits and sugar mix. Whisk the butter and eggs until light and foamy. Fold this into the fruit, nut and sugar mixture. Add the honey. Gently fold all the ingredients together until the mixture is lovely and shiny.

Pour the doughy mixture into the cake tin and bake for about 50 minutes or until a skewer comes out clean. Allow the cake to cool slightly before removing it from the tin. Place the cake on a stand and, if you want to, sprinkle a little sweet sherry or even some brandy onto the still-warm cake. Decorate with the lovely glacé fruit and serve with thick cream.

RIGHT: *Clyde Road, Green Point Village*
MIDDLE: *Cobbled street in front of*
St Margaret Mary's.
AR RIGHT: *The Food Studio kitchen table.*

Poulet à la Lyonnaise

A classic Parisian bistro dish.

Serves 4

- 250 g tomatoes, peeled, de-seeded and chopped
- 1 large chicken
- 125 ml butter
- 2 T flour
- 1 T white wine vinegar
- 125 ml dry white wine
- 175 ml fresh cream
- sea salt and freshly ground black pepper
- baby potatoes, peeled and steamed, to serve
- 4 cloves garlic, chopped, to serve
- 1 T butter, melted, to serve

Cook the tomatoes in a small pot for about 10 minutes. Remove from the heat and keep warm.

Cut the chicken into eight pieces.

Heat the butter in a saucepan. Toss the chicken pieces in the flour and drop into the hot butter. Brown lightly on all sides, then lower the heat, cover and cook slowly for 15 minutes. Season.

Add the vinegar to the pan, and scrape around the bottom to lift all the sticky bits. Then add the wine and stir well. Add the cream and the tomatoes. Mix well, cover and allow to simmer for about 10 minutes or until chicken is cooked through. Taste and season.

Serve hot with gently steamed baby potatoes. Garnish them with a handful of freshly chopped raw garlic stirred into the tablespoon of melted butter.

LEFT: *Road sign in Clyde Road, Green Point.*
RIGHT: *Fun trompe l'oeil mural in Clyde Road.*

STUDIO IN GREEN POINT

GREENPOINT'S BEST KEPT SECRET!*

Fig & nut cake

WITH CREAMY COFFEE ICING

When my son was small, we used to bake a cake every Friday afternoon. This was an absolute favourite.

Serves 10

- 125 ml butter
- 500 ml sugar
- 2 eggs
- 375 g self-raising flour
- 1 t salt
- 1 t cinnamon
- ¼ t ground cloves
- 125 ml milk
- 500 g dried figs, lightly stewed in 250 ml water and chopped into small cubes
- 125 ml chopped walnuts
- 2 t vanilla paste

COFFEE ICING
- 750 g icing sugar, sifted
- pinch salt
- 125 g softened butter
- 1 T coffee essence
- 1 T milk
- 1 t vanilla paste

Preheat the oven to 180 deg C/Gas 4.

Cream the butter and sugar until light in colour. Add the eggs one at a time, and beat well. Sift all the dry ingredients together and fold into the egg mixture, alternating with the leftover liquid from the stewed figs and the milk. Fold in the figs, walnuts and vanilla paste. Pour into a buttered cake tin and bake for about 80 minutes or until a skewer comes out clean.

Remove from the oven and allow to rest a little before turning the cake out onto a rack to cool down.

When the cake is cold, make the icing. Beat the icing sugar, butter, coffee essence, milk and vanilla together until smooth and creamy, and spread over the cake.

Enjoy with a glass of cool, sweet wine.

RIGHT: *"Come in and gossip …"*
FAR RIGHT: *The best-kept secret in Green Point Village.*

STUDIO IN GREEN POINT

CHAPTER 9

Middens & vines

Climbing to the top of a 2000-year-old shell midden to lay a table for a feast at the southernmost tip of Africa was one of the most wonderful things I've done in years.

After the meal, we went for a walk down the wild, endless beach, with only seagulls and a couple of Black Oystercatchers for company. Later, back at the ancient stone and thatch homestead, we sat down to a chilled glass of First Sighting Sauvignon Blanc from the Strandveld Vineyards.

The previous day we had driven through the lush green vines of this Cape Agulhas farm, quite taken by the beauty of the indigenous fynbos, proteas and birds. On the horizon, the blue of the sea. We tasted the wines in the cellar, and found them full of the promise one hopes for from new frontiers.

Later in the day we sat down to a leisurely lunch of tomatoes, basil pesto and melted Gorgonzola, fresh fish and roasted peppers. Simple fare that reminds one that where earth and ocean meet, there lies the magic. 👑

- Mozzarella salad with anchovies & capers — 173
- Seared tuna with pistou, tomatoes & black olives — 175
- Toasted tomatoes with pesto & Gorgonzola — 177
- Raan — 179
- Ricotta dessert with cognac & citrus zest — 181
- Asparagus with white anchovies — 183
- Red roman on the embers — 185
- Strawberries with Hanepoot — 187

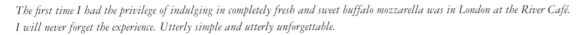 Mozzarella salad
WITH ANCHOVIES & CAPERS

The first time I had the privilege of indulging in completely fresh and sweet buffalo mozzarella was in London at the River Café. I will never forget the experience. Utterly simple and utterly unforgettable.

Serves 2

- 250 g fresh buffalo mozzarella
- 2 T extra virgin olive oil
- 1 t well-aged balsamic vinegar
- 1 t excellent mustard ... I'm really partial to the mustard from Charroux
- 1 T small capers
- 6 small white achovies
- 1 T fennel leaves, finely chopped
- sea salt and freshly ground black pepper to taste

Allow the buffalo mozzarella to rest outside the fridge until it reaches room temperature. In a small bowl, lightly whisk the olive oil, balsamic vinegar and mustard together. Toss the capers into the vinaigrette. Using your fingers, shred the mozzarella onto a serving dish, and spoon the caper mixture over the cheese. Arrange the white anchovies prettily on top and lightly garnish with the chopped fennel leaves. Season to taste and serve with a piece of warm, crusty bread and a glass of white wine.

ABOVE: *The view of the stone and thatch homestead from across the beach.*
FAR LEFT: *'Sewejaartjies' (forget-me-nots) growing on the midden.*

MIDDENS & VINES

Sepia memories.

Seared tuna

WITH PISTOU, TOMATOES & BLACK OLIVES

The first time I tasted tuna cooked this way was at the waterfront restaurant, Atmosphere, next to the Allier River in Vichy. We've been back many times ... Ideally one would throw these wonderful thickly cut fillets onto an open, red-hot grill. Preferably with some real flames licking at them!

Serves 4

- 4 × 250 g fresh tuna steaks, thickly cut
- flesh of 4 ripe tomatoes, peeled and de-seeded
- 20 black olives, stoned

For the pistou:
- 3 cloves garlic
- leaves from 1 bunch basil
- 100 ml extra virgin olive oil
- 8 anchovies

With this dish it is necessary to prepare the pistou* first. Place the garlic, basil, olive oil and anchovies in a food processor and blend to a rough paste. Grill the fish at a very high heat until it is completely seared on all sides but still pink and succulent inside.

Spoon the pistou into a small bowl, add the tomatoes and olives, and gently fold together.

Place the smoking-hot fish on individual plates and spoon the pistou mixture over the fish. Serve immediately with a green salad.

* *A pistou is a cold sauce often made by pounding the ingredients together using a pestle and mortar – but the food processor does a good job of it too.*

ABOVE LEFT: *For whom the bell tolls ... in this case to summon plates filled with food!*
ABOVE RIGHT: *Driftwood woven into a chandelier.*

"One of the very nicest things about life is the way in which we must regularly stop with whatever it is we are doing and devote our attention to eating."

Luciano Pavarotti

Toasted tomatoes
WITH PESTO & GORGONZOLA

This is a great starter for a fish barbeque. And you eat this with your fingers, naturally.

Serves 6

- 6 plum tomatoes, halved
- salt and freshly ground black pepper
- 150 ml olive oil
- 200 g Gorgonzola, crumbled
- 12 slices of baguette, lightly toasted
- 125 ml basil pesto
- basil leaves, to serve

Place the tomato halves onto an oiled baking tray. Season lightly and drizzle a little olive oil over them. Grill for about 5 minutes before adding a sprinkling of Gorgonzola over each tomato. Return to the oven and allow the cheese to melt and cook slightly.

Arrange the little toasted slices of bread on individual plates, and place the hot tomatoes on top. Spoon a teaspoon of pesto on top of each one. Scatter the basil leaves over them and dress with the rest of the olive oil and a little black pepper.

Serve immediately.

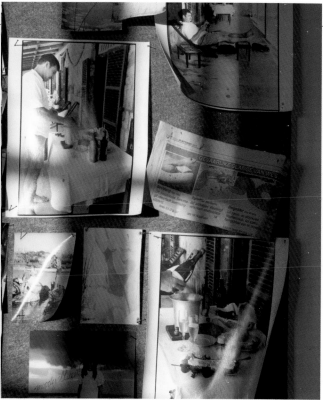

Old pictures of old friends.

"Wine can of the wits beguile,

make the sage frolic,

and the serious smile."

Homer

MIDDENS & VINES

Raan

This Hyderabadi recipe is rich and aromatic, and is a favourite of the Food Studio as a result of my friend, Eleanor. She wrote it down many years ago ... took me ages to decipher the faded pencil markings! Hyderabadi cuisine is based on the traditional method of combining sour, sweet, hot and salty, and has been extensively influenced by various Indian regional and religious cuisines.

Serves 8 comfortably

- 1 leg of lamb, trimmed
- 5 T lemon juice, freshly squeezed
- rind of 2 lemons
- 125 g fresh root ginger, peeled and chopped
- 10 large cloves garlic, peeled and chopped
- 1 t turmeric
- 2 t cumin
- 6 cardamom pods, de-seeded
- 2 t dried chilli
- ½ t cinnamon
- 3 t sea salt
- 3 bay leaves
- 2 star anise
- 250 g powdered almonds
- 4 T brown sugar
- 500 ml thick, full-cream yoghurt
- ½ t saffron strands, soaked in 2 T boiling water

Use a small sharp knife to make several deep gashes in the leg of lamb.

Use a pestle and mortar to blend the lemon juice, rind, ginger, garlic, turmeric, cumin, cardamom, chilli, cinnamon and salt thoroughly until a thick purée forms. Take a spatula and spread the purée thickly over the entire leg of lamb. Stick the bay leaves and star anise to the meat. Place the covered meat in the fridge for about an hour.

Put the almonds, sugar and half of the yoghurt into an electric blender and purée at high speed. Scrape the almond paste into a mixing bowl and fold the remaining yoghurt into the paste. Remove the lamb from the fridge and spoon the almond paste over the spicy coating. Cover the lamb and return to the fridge for another 48 hours.

Remove the lamb from the fridge about 2 hours before cooking time to allow the meat to reach room temperature before going into the oven. Heat the oven to 220 deg C/Gas 7 and roast the leg of lamb for 20 minutes. Turn the temperature down to 180 deg C/Gas 4 and cover the meat before returning it to the oven for another 3 hours. Once the meat is cooked and tender, remove it from the oven pan and place it on a serving platter. Remove all excess fat from the pan before pouring the juices into a cooking pot. Add the saffron to the stock and bring to a rapid boil, until the meat juices reduce to become a lovely sauce. Slice the lamb, spoon the sauce over it, and serve with couscous.

RIGHT: *The crisp Strandveld wines.*

MIDDENS & VINES

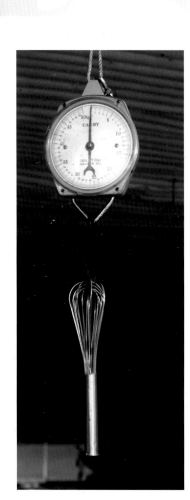

Winemaker's tools!

Ricotta dessert
WITH COGNAC & CITRUS ZEST

I read this recipe years ago in a magazine. And it was attributed to a gentleman named Ron. Thanks Ron!

Serves 6

- 250 g castor sugar
- 75 ml water
- 250 ml cognac
- zest of 1 lemon, 1 lime and 1 orange
- 1 t vanilla paste
- 1 whole ricotta, about 500 g
- 100 g pistachio nuts, lightly roasted

Use a small cooking pot and melt the sugar in the water. Add the cognac and the three types of zest, and reduce over a low heat until they are beautifully glazed and translucent. Take care that the mixture does not reduce too much and crystallise. Add a little water if necessary. Stir the vanilla into the syrup.

Place the whole ricotta on a slightly hollow serving plate and spoon the syrup over the cheese. Arrange the glistening zest on top and toss the pistachio nuts over the cheese just before serving.

Lovely with an oat biscuit and, of course, a snifter of cognac or brandy.

LEFT: *The Strandveld cellar close to Cape L'Agulhas.*
MIDDLE: *First fill oak with Pinot Noir.*
RIGHT: *Inside the wine-tasting room.*

Red roman
ON THE EMBERS

A privilege we are still truly lucky to experience, is that of putting a freshly caught fish on a wood fire right next to the sea. Simply done, with some roasted red peppers on the side ...

One fish will be enough for 4 people to enjoy

- 1 red roman, cleaned
- 50 ml olive oil
- juice and zest of 1 lemon
- 1 clove garlic, crushed
- 50 g butter
- salt and freshly ground black pepper
- 2 red peppers*

Rub the skin of the roman ... why do I love this line? ... with the olive oil and place in a folding grill over moderate coals.

Grill fast, but gently and turn the fish regularly. Once the flesh starts to turn white, it is cooked. Remove from the coals, and brush with a mixture of lemon juice, zest, butter and fresh garlic. Season and serve with the peppers and some sweet potatoes.

*Place the red peppers on the grill next to the fish and roast all round until the skins have blackened. Remove from the fire, allow to cool and peel, removing the little pips with your fingers as you go. Slice in thick slivers, season lightly and serve with the fish.

ABOVE: *The very best way ...*
LEFT: *Lone fisherman.*

MIDDENS & VINES

k-Cooker"
MEDAL–LONDON 191!
NT FOR STEWS OF ALL KINDS
N BE KEPT HOT FOR HOURS
R–COOKING OR GETTING DRY
RIMWADE'S

Strawberries

WITH HANEPOOT

And how good is this! If you cannot get your hands on some Hanepoot, use a sweet, mature sherry.

- 500 g ripe strawberries, trimmed and sliced
- 50 g icing sugar
- 250 ml Hanepoot
- ½ t matured balsamic vinegar
- freshly ground black pepper
- 350 ml rich, thick yoghurt
- 150 ml golden honey

Place the strawberries in a mixing bowl and sprinkle the icing sugar over them. Allow to rest until the icing sugar has melted away. Add the Hanepoot and the balsamic vinegar to the bowl, and leave the strawberries to soak for at least an hour. Spoon the strawberries into individual serving bowls and give each bowl a sprinkling of black pepper. Add a dollop of yoghurt to each portion and garnish with a dribble of honey before serving. Delicious!

RIGHT: *On top of the 2 000-year-old midden.*

MIDDENS & VINES

CHAPTER 10

Goddesses & ghosts

In the beautiful narrow and verdant Wamakers Valley, between the Seven Sisters and the Hawequa, lies the old wine farm, De Compagnie. It has only slightly restless ghosts, and a long line of female owners contributing to the rich, spicy past of this lovely old homestead and ancient kitchen.

Lady Anne Barnard eloquently described a feast prepared here in her Cape Journals – and one wonders what other dinners have come from this massive hearth.

This could not be the first time a nourishing harvest soup steamed in the cool, dark kitchen. And what distant wind rustled up the urge among these modern women to turn a hand to the kind of alchemy that conjures up, out of an old Chenin Blanc vineyard, this deep old-gold ambrosia in the crystal goblet I'm holding in my hand?

After the fruit of the vines has been doubly distilled in the mid-19th century copper alambic, just the heart of the golden goddess – brandy – is held in oak barrels for a whole decade of peace and absolute quiet before she is gently released to sensually flaunt her fiery soul …

We knew, on that blistering summer's day, taking small sips of this liquid, redolent of sun-warmed figs and creamy spices, that we were utterly seduced. ♕

- La soupe des vendanges — 191
- Beef tongue with caper berries & black olives — 193
- Blueberry pie — 195
- Venison fillet pan-fried with ginger & sage — 197
- Sweet potatoes with ginger & chillies — 199
- Poppy seed & orange cake — 201
- Creamy chicken with rosemary — 203
- Fabulous coffee cake — 205

La soupe des vendanges

This french winemakers' soup could easily be served to the harvesters in the Cape vineyards as well. After a long, hard day of backbreaking work, a feisty soup is called for.

Serves 8

- 4 T extra virgin olive oil
- 4 leeks, sliced in pennies and washed
- 2 medium carrots, peeled and sliced in pennies
- 4 medium potatoes, peeled and sliced
- 250 g haricot beans
- 4 cloves garlic, peeled and chopped
- 350 g pork belly, diced
- 1 shoulder of springbok, whole with bone
- 3 × 10 cm marrow bones – ask your butcher!
- 1 fattened duck
- 2 bottles of dry white wine
- 2 l water
- bouquet garni
- salt and freshly ground black pepper

ABOVE LEFT: *Farm produce to use in a fabulous soup.* ABOVE RIGHT: *Old glassware in the diningroom.*

For this soup I use the biggest pot I can lay my hands on – in Charroux it's usually the ancient Rosieres I found in a brocante in a village close to Vichy; in the Cape, a little more prosaic, it's a 24-litre I bought from the local chef's shop. Heat the olive oil and gently braise the leeks, carrots, potatoes, beans, garlic and pork belly until the leeks are translucent but not browned. Add the springbok, marrow bones and duck to the pot. Cover with the wine and water, and bring to the boil. Reduce the heat to a simmer and add the bouquet garni.

After about 2 hours, you can remove the venison, duck and marrow bones from the pot and debone the meat. I use my fingers (after the meat has cooled down a little!) to shred the meat in smallish pieces before returning it to the soup. At this point you can skim some fat from the soup. Allow the soup to reduce enough to be fairly thick, season and then serve it in hearty portions with a dollop of aioli and a warm, crusty slice of bread.

*"Kissing don't last;
cookery do!"*
George Meredith

Window sill and hob in the kitchen of De Compagnie.

GODDESSES & GHOSTS

Beef tongue
WITH CAPER BERRIES & BLACK OLIVES

This was one of those accidental recipes that just happened one evening when some friends arrived unexpectedly. It's delicious though, and I've repeated it often.

Serves 4

- 1 beef tongue, cooked,* peeled and sliced into thinnish slivers
- 250 ml cream
- 2 t honey
- 1 T walnut oil
- 1 T smooth French mustard
- 100 g caper berries
- 250 g black olives, stoned

Place the slices of beef tongue on a serving platter, allowing them to overlap slightly. Keep warm.

In a small mixing bowl, whisk together the cream, honey, walnut oil and mustard. It will blend into a yummy, thick sauce. Scatter the caper berries and olives over the slices of tongue before spooning the sauce over the still-warm meat.

Serve immediately with some fruity white wine.

*To cook a pickled beef tongue, you need a large pot with enough water to cover the meat comfortably. Add a glass of dry white wine to the water just for effect ... and drink one! Add about 6 cloves to the water, as well as a bay leaf or two. A few whole peppercorns aren't a bad idea either.
Bring the liquid to a slow boil and keep that going until the meat is absolutely tender. About 2 hours should do it. Allow the meat to cool down slightly before peeling it. You don't want to burn your fingers! Slice and serve.

A corner with vegetables next to the stove.

GODDESSES & GHOSTS

Blueberry pie

This is a deceptively easy pie to make. I enjoy the way the glossy berries pop in one's mouth when you bite into them!

Serves 8

- 1 roll puff pastry, defrosted
- 1 kg fresh blueberries
- 3 eggs
- 3 T castor sugar
- 200 ml cream

Preheat the oven to 220 deg C/Gas 6.

Roll the pastry to fit a 23 cm pie plate or individual moulds. Butter the pie plate or moulds, and line them with the pastry. Beat the eggs with the sugar and fold in the cream. Fill the pastry with the blueberries and pour the creamy mixture over the berries. Bake for about 25 minutes or until the filling has set.

Allow to cool and serve with a dollop of cream.

"Shape is a good part of the fig's delight ..."
Jane Grigson

Venison fillet pan-fried
WITH GINGER & SAGE

A great way to cook a kudu or gemsbuck fillet on top of the stove. Girls don't always feel like a fire!

Serves 8

- 2 T extra virgin olive oil
- 1 medium carrot, peeled and sliced in pennies
- 1 sweet brown onion, peeled and finely chopped
- 2 cloves garlic, peeled and chopped
- 100 g pancetta, diced
- 1 tiny thumb fresh ginger, peeled and chopped
- 2 small red chillies, de-seeded and chopped
- 1 large venison fillet, cleaned
- 2 bay leaves
- 6 sprigs parsley
- 2 T fresh sage leaves, chopped
- 4 sprigs rosemary, chopped
- 250 ml dry red wine
- salt and freshly ground black pepper to taste

Heat the olive oil in a large pan and add the carrot, onion, garlic, pancetta, ginger and chillies. Fry gently until the pancetta is browned. Add the fillet to the pan and brown properly over a low heat. This should take about 10 minutes. Add all the herbs and cook for a minute or two before removing the fillet from the pan. Deglaze with the wine, scraping all the bits from the bottom and the sides of the pan. If necessary, add some more wine and reduce the liquid until you have a lovely sauce.

Cut the fillet in portions and return to the pan to reheat in the pan juices before serving. Season and serve with all the bits and pieces spooned over the meat.

Serve with a handful of crisp rocket from your garden and a sprinkling of freshly chopped sage and parsley.

FAR LEFT: *'Objets' on the huge stoep.*
ABOVE RIGHT: *Vineyards in the Wellington valley.*

Sweet potatoes
WITH GINGER & CHILLIES

Something zesty to add to your plate whenever you are indulging in a fillet of venison.

Serves 8

- 750 g sweet potatoes, peeled and cubed
- 125 ml olive oil
- 75 g butter, cut in tiny blocks
- 200 ml sugar
- 2 fingers of fresh ginger, peeled and chopped
- 2 red chillies, de-seeded and chopped
- 6 salad onions, chopped

Place the sweet potatoes in an oven dish, drizzle with the olive oil and scatter the butter blocks over them. Bake in a hot oven, 200 deg C/Gas 6, for about an hour.

Remove the pan from the oven, drain the juices into a small pot, add the sugar, chopped ginger and chillies, and bring to the boil. You can add a little water if you do not have enough liquid.

Allow the sugar to melt and the sauce to reach a syrupy consistency. Spoon over the still-warm sweet potatoes, garnish with the salad onions and enjoy!

RIGHT: *Cupboards filled with heirlooms.*

Poppy seed & orange cake

Another family favourite that has its regular place in the 'What cake do we have for the weekend?' line-up.

Serves 8

- 125 g butter
- 250 g castor sugar
- 2 eggs
- zest of 1 large lemon
- 375 ml self-raising flour
- 125 ml milk
- 2 t vanilla paste
- 1 t cinnamon
- 125 ml poppy seeds

SERIOUS SYRUP

- juice of 1 lemon
- 250 ml castor sugar
- 250 ml water
- zest of 2 oranges, julienned
- zest of 2 lemons, julienned
- zest of 2 limes, julienned

Butter and flour a round cake tin and preheat the oven to 180 deg C/ Gas 4.

It is also a good idea to line the tin with a round of wax paper if you feel like it.

Cream the butter and sugar before adding the eggs one at a time. Beat well. Stir in the zest, flour, milk, vanilla, cinnamon and poppy seeds, and mix really well. Spoon the dough into the cake tin and bake for about 35 minutes or until a skewer comes out clean. Allow the cake to rest for a while before turning it out onto a wire rack to cool down.

To make the syrup, combine the lemon juice, castor sugar and water in a small pot. Bring to a gentle boil and allow the sugar to melt before adding all the zest. Keep reducing the liquid until it is wonderfully syrupy and the zests are completely glazed and almost see-through.

Place the cake on a serving platter and spoon the very warm syrup over it. To decorate, pile the zest in a heap in the middle of the cake.

FAR LEFT: *Pewter and camomile.*

RIGHT: *Shaded verandah reminiscent of previous lives.*

Creamy chicken with rosemary

This is one of those comfortable, 'must-have' recipes … one you make when you're feeling slightly low and in need of some nurturing.

Serves 4

- 2 T extra virgin olive oil
- 50 g butter
- 1 medium chicken, cut in portions
- 1 stick of celery, washed and chopped (leaves and all)
- 2 leeks, sliced in pennies and washed
- 6 long sprigs of rosemary, rolled tightly in two leek leaves
- 500 ml chicken stock
- 250 ml cream
- 50 ml dry sherry
- salt and freshly ground black pepper

Heat the olive oil in a pan, melt the butter into it and quick-fry the chicken until lightly browned.

Add the celery, leeks, rosemary and stock. Allow the broth to simmer gently until the chicken is cooked to perfection – almost falling off the bone. And please add more stock if it is needed! Remove the chicken from the pan and keep warm.

Add the cream and reduce the sauce until it is lovely and thick. Remove the rosemary bouquet garni. Stir the sherry into the cream sauce, pour over the chicken, season to taste and garnish with a fresh sprig of rosemary.

Utterly satisfying.

ABOVE: *The stuff that kitchens are made of.*
FAR LEFT: *Peach-pip floor in the cool kitchen.*

GODDESSES & GHOSTS

*"Don't just talk about
a good brandy. Sip it
with esteem and do
not rush."
My father*

FABULOUS
Coffee cake

This is my favourite cake. And one my dear mother had to make on my birthday every year ... that is, after the specially requested bowl of tripe! No logic whatsoever.

- 200 g butter
- 250 ml castor sugar
- 3 eggs
- 375 ml self-raising flour
- pinch of salt
- 100 ml sugar
- 250 ml strong black coffee
- cognac to taste
- 5 ml vanilla paste
- 250 ml thick cream
- handful of almonds, flaked and lightly roasted

Grease a ring form or normal cake tin (20 cm) and pre-heat the oven to 190 deg C/Gas 5. In a blender, cream the butter and castor sugar until light and airy. Add the eggs one at a time and beat in thoroughly. Gently fold the flour and salt into the mixture. Spoon into the cake tin and bake for about 30 minutes or until a skewer comes out clean. Remove from the oven and allow to rest a couple of minutes before tipping onto a cooling rack.

In a pan, dissolve the sugar in the coffee and add the cognac to taste. Place the cooled cake on a cake stand and gently pour the coffee syrup over the cake, completely drenching it. Combine the vanilla and cream and whip until peaks form. Spoon over the coffee cake and garnish with the almonds. You might be tempted to enjoy this with a small tumbler of cognac!

INDEX

BEEF

Beef fillet	93
Beef tongue with caper berries & black olives	193
Entrecôte Beaujolaise	13
Pot au feu with roasted potatoes & rosemary	71
Veal cutlets with salsa verde	17

BREAKFAST

Muesli from the Food Studio	159
Salmon & egg pots	145

CHICKEN

Chicken with pancetta, preserved lemon & herbs	147
Chicken with white wine, black olives & flambéed baby onions	77
Creamy chicken with rosemary	203
Crêtes & roupettes	67
Poulet à la Lyonnaise	167
Une poule dans son pot	39

DESSERT – CAKE

Autumn cake with berries	85
Fabulous coffee cake	205
Fig & nut cake with creamy coffee icing	169
Pistachio cake with Noble Late Harvest wine	123
Poppy seed & orange cake	201
Tea cake with glazed fruits	164

DESSERT – OTHER

Blinis Aux Jardins des Thévenets	133
Cassis sorbet with ripe cherries	57
Champagne jelly with berries	105
Champagne sabayon	129
Chocolate pots	79
Luxe apple pies in custard crust	41
Malva pudding	113
Orange pudding from Ouma Mollie	157
Ricotta dessert with cognac & citrus zest	181
Roly-poly with apricot confit	25
Soufflé Grand Marnier	65
Strawberries with Hanepoot	187
White peach & basil compote	101

DESSERT – TARTS & PIES

Blueberry pie	195
Cherry clafoutis	15
Grape & fennel seed tart	139
Tarte au citron	149

FISH & OTHER SEAFOOD

Poached salmon with soubise	125
Red roman on the embers	185
Sardines oven-roasted	97
Seared tuna with pistou, tomatoes & black olives	175
White fish with black olives & saffron sauce	163

LAMB

French lamb shanks with tomato & Gorgonzola cream	131
Lamb ribs with puy lentils & prosciutto	118
Pan-fried lamb cutlets with Gruyère	83
Raan	179
Spicy shoulder of lamb with aubergine caviar	53
Tomato and lamb stew ancienne	111

PORK

Cassoulet	86
Pork belly with star anise, cider & honey	23

SALAD

Buffalo mozzarella with tomato	137
Chicken livers with prosciutto & roasted baby potato salad	45
Mozzarella salad with anchovies & capers	173
Potato, bean & prosciutto salad	109

SOUP

Butternut & leek soup	59
Chestnut & mushroom soup	21
Chilled tomato soup	116
French onion soup	11
La soupe des vendanges	191
Spinach & sorrel soup	153
Tomato, chickpea & lentil soup	141

STARTERS & SIDE DISHES

Asparagus with white anchovies	183
Aubergine caviar	54
Carrots with roasted walnuts in orange juice	33
Chicken liver pâté with port jelly	51
Couscous with fresh parsley	121
Endive with fennel & thyme	127
Fresh figs with prosciutto & Roquefort cream	161
Green beans with anchovies & almonds	37
Melanzane Parmigiana	107
Potato & paprika bake	19
Puy lentils with prosciutto	119
Ripe pears smothered in tarragon hollandaise	81
Sweet potatoes with ginger & chillies	199
Toasted tomatoes with pesto & Gorgonzola	177

TARTS & PIES – SAVOURY

Butternut & chèvre tartlets with pine nuts	69
Classic quiche Lorraine	47
English pot pies à la David	89
Goat's cheese tarts with hazelnuts	75
Pâté aux pommes des terre	35
Pissaladière	43
Terrine de campagne	31

VENISON

Duck breasts with green olive tapenade	103
Lapin with saucisson, sage & smashed potatoes	61
Quail with prosciutto & sage	99
Succulent duck with ginger, chillies & coconut milk	155
Venison fillet pan-fried with ginger & sage	197
Venison tagliatelle	143

Sumptuous © **Marlene van der Westhuizen** and **Gerda Genis**, 2009

ISBN: 978-1-920075-91-0

This first edition jointly published by Rollerbird Press, a division of Troupant Publishers (Pty) Limited, P O Box 4532, Northcliff, 2115, South Africa
and
Pan Macmillan South Africa a division of Macmillan SA (Pty) Limited, Private Bag X19, Northlands, 2116, South Africa

Distributed by Pan Macmillan South Africa (Pty) Ltd, via Booksite Africa

Edited by Heather Parker and Pat Botes, proofread by Salome Smit and Mark McClellan, cover design and layout by Gerda Genis, repro by Colour Extreme, printed and bound by Ultra Litho (Pty) Limited

GLOSSARY

aioli: garlic mayonnaise

al dente: still slightly chewy, not too soft

al fresco: in the fresh air, outside

ancienne: ancient

au gratin: baked or browned with breadcrumbs

baguette: a flute-shaped loaf of French bread

bain marie: pan with simmering water with a bowl suspended in it

béchamel: white sauce made with butter, flour, milk and seasoning

beurre noisette: butter that has been gently heated in a frying pan until it is a dark golden colour and gives off a nutty smell

blanch: bring water to a boil, add ingredients and bring to the boil for no more that 2 minutes

boulangerie: bakery

bouquet garni: a selection of aromatic herbs and plants, tied together in a small bundle and used to add flavour to sauces and stocks

brasserie luxe: bistro food presented luxuriously

brocante: antique market

charcuterie: cooked or cured meat products

chèvre: cheese made from goat's milk

confit: piece of meat cooked in its own fat and stored. Covered in its own fat to preserve it

confit de canard: duck cooked slowly in its own fat and stored covered by its own fat

coulis: a liquid puree of fruit

crème anglaise: custard

crème fraîche: a cream to which a lactic acid has been added which thickens the cream, and gives it a distinctive sharp flavour without souring the cream

creperie: small restaurant specialising in crepes

crête: cockscomb

de campagne: countryside

deglaze: adding a drop of wine to a used pan and scraping all the bits and pieces full of flavour together before producing a magnificent sauce

demerara sugar: light brown cane sugar

dollop: scoop

emulsify: to combine two or more liquids (e.g. eggs, oil and lemon juice) in such a way that they are equally dispersed in each other and produce an emulsion (e.g. mayonnaise)

entrecote: rib steak

epicerie: grocer's

escalope: thinnish slice of meat

flambé: to flame with cognac or other alcohol

foie gras a la grandmere: liver cooked as my grandmother used to

glace: frozen, iced

gremolata: a mixture of chopped parsley, garlic and lemon peel

jus de caisson: natural juices or gravy

lapin: rabbit

pissaladière: French type of pizza

pistou: pesto

poach: lightly boil in wine or water

pulse: intermittent beating (as in 'mix')

purée: creaming cooked foods through a sieve or with a food processor

ragout: a stew made from meat, poultry, game, fish or vegetables that is cooked in a thickened liquid and flavoured with herbs and seasonings

reduce: to concentrate or thicken a sauce or soup by boiling

roupettes: cocks' oysters

roux: equal amounts of butter and flour used to make or thicken sauces

roux brun: same as above but cooked longer until it has browned slightly

sabayon: light foam made by whisking egg yolks, wine and sugar together over a gentle heat

saucisses de Toulouse: sausages from Toulouse

saucisson: sausage

saucisson à cuire: cooked sausage

sorbet: a water-ice that is softer and more granular than ice cream

soupçon: a very small amount of something; the merest hint

terrine: a mix of chopped vegetables, meats and flavourings pressed into a container, cooked and served cold

truss: to tie

velouté: a basic sauce made with chicken or veal stock and thickened with a roux

---

ACKNOWLEDGEMENTS

I wrote *Sumptuous* for my dear friend, Deon, and our fabulous son, Renier.

I thank the following people with all my heart and in the complete knowledge that no one can write a book without massive and total support.

Firstly, Gerda Genis, who is the most astonishing, warmest and kindest photographer I've ever worked with. What a privilege to have collaborated on this project with you.

Marie-Chantal Bardet, David and Colleen Sharpe, Sylviane Meunier, Olivier and Lynn Chaulieu, Christof and LZ Albertyn, and Riana Scheepers and her winged words –
thanks for opening your homes, farms and hearts.

I have to thank Anna-marie Remington-Hobbs and Dawie Weideman for the heaps of linen, silver, dishes, pots and pans that were washed, sun-bleached, polished and scrubbed. You were fantastic!

To my housekeeper and friend, Joyce Melane ... I agree, three months in France was pushing it a bit. Thank you so much for looking after me and mine.

And Heather Parker, thanks for copy-editing this one as well. To Mike Lancaster who did the repro and colour managment – thank you.

Basil van Rooyen and Terry Morris who agreed once again to publish a book of mine. Thank you so much. Thank you Lindsey Cohen. Editing and proofreading were never meant to be funny.

My long-suffering family and all our friends who had to test-eat endless meals deserve a bucketful of hugs. Thanks for your support.

To the young gentleman I share my life with – Renier, you did a splendid job with your matric exam. Thanks, you did well.

And Deon, let's run away to Paris for a lifetime of jazz ...

Marlene van der Westhuizen